Living the Mystery

First published in 2019
by Columba Books
23 Merrion Square North,
Dublin 2, Co. Dublin
www.columbabooks.com

ISBN: 978-1-78218-356-3

Set in Adobe Garamond Pro 11/15
Cover and book design by Alba Esteban | Columba Books
Printed by ScandBook, Sweden

Living the Mystery

MARK PATRICK HEDERMAN

columba
BOOKS

For
Sacha Abercorn
and
Pegasus
Bright Stars of Our Firmament

CONTENTS

INTRODUCTION

There is a way to live our lives in and through mystery. It is different from other ways of travelling from birth to death. As things are, many of us hardly ever get into the driving seat. Our parents, our teachers, those in charge, arrange the trajectory and set the pace. We go to school, we end up in a profession, we take a job, we get married, we draw a pension, we die. In between we have pastimes, hobbies, extracurricular interests, for which we shore up whatever time is left over, but we never really live in a groove that satisfies.

Such is life as career. There is a map, a set of rules, a beginning, a number of goals and an end. Career guidance will tell you how to fit yourself into this scheme of things. Your talents, your prospects, your cultural baggage will be weighed and assessed in terms of your capacity to slot into wherever you might fit most profitably and most comfortably on the conveyor belt. Life in this perspective is a set of problems to be analysed, squared up to and overcome. There is no mystery about it. You examine the cards you were dealt when you arrived, and you play your hand as astutely as you can. Who knows, you might even hit the jackpot. This would mean, basically, health, wealth and recognition. You become a model for all those young aspirants towards success, as this is defined and recognised in the socio-economic world in which we live.

And such accomplishment is nowadays, in theory at any rate, open and available to any of the over seven billion inhabitants of the planet. In times past, your gender, your position on the social ladder, or the colour of your skin might automatically exclude you from reaching the top; but in this 21st Century everything is potentially possible for everyone. Even though some might legitimately argue that such barriers still exist in many parts of the world, the pitches have certainly become more levelled and the general overall aspiration is towards equal opportunity for all. So, we can all play the game by placing our bets and rolling the dice.

And, if, just supposing, we managed to divide up the wealth of our planet in such a way that everyone had sufficient food and equal opportunity, then, and only then, would the real problem of human existence emerge. Having struggled to assert ourselves and having overcome the obstacles in our way, having arrived at some kind of equilibrium and wellbeing, what then? Is this all we had to live for? Having settled all the problems of human rights, balance of power, oppression and injustice, where would we be in terms of fulfilment and satisfying outcomes? Is, at the very most, 100 years of wellbeing on this planet sufficient to satisfy our fundamental yearnings and desire?

But, suppose for a moment that there is another way of playing the game, of living our lives from birth to death and beyond. Supposing that life is not just a problem to be negotiated, but rather a mystery quite beyond the comprehension of our normal ways of understanding. What would be the point of wringing our hands and refusing to play because the rules we discover are not to our liking? No point in saying at the end of the game that we thought we were playing croquet when in fact we were meant to be playing darts. We didn't throw the party or invent the game in the first place. It is not for us to insist that the regulations we anticipated should be observed.

Let us agree that there must be at least two ways of living our lives from birth to death on this planet of ours. We all live in the inside of our heads and such constriction can lead us to imagine that everyone else in the world sees things as we do. It comes as a surprise to find that others see things quite differently, that the inside of each one's head is a different country.

I found this out one day while I was teaching. I was explaining to a class of teenagers how to write an essay. "Don't be boring and predictable," I said, "Use your imaginations. If the subject of your essay is 'jeans' for instance, don't give an account of the industry, the history, the way they are made. Find something outrageous, something that will wake the reader up. Tell them that 'jeans' is from the French for John – that 'long johns' are a close relative; that we borrow from other vocabularies whenever words gain universal currency. That's why 'biftek' is now a word in French for what we serve as 'beef steak'. If you happen to say: 'Au contraire, on Mardi Gras, the entrepreneurial chef served an à la carte omelette, comme ci comme ça, RSVP'; you're actually speaking French." I looked around the room enthusiastically. Glazed eyeballs met my gaze. "Okay," I said, "each one of you is going to write down in one single paragraph what I have just said to you." One boy handed me: "Jeans is the French for beef steak." He wasn't joking. That's the way what I had said entered his head. That was the day I learned that my mind works differently from other minds on the planet.

TWO TRAVELLERS
By Cecil Day Lewis

One of us in the compartment stares
Out of his window the whole day long
With attentive mien, as if he knows,
There is hid in the journeying scene a song
To recall or compose
From snatches of vision, hints of vanishing airs.

The other is plainly a man of affairs,
A seasoned commuter. His looks assert,
As he opens a briefcase intent on perusing
Facts and figures, he'd never divert
With profitless musing
The longest journey, or notice the dress it wears.

One is preoccupied, one just stares,
While the whale-ribbed terminus nears apace
Where passengers all must change, and under
Its arch triumphal quickly disperse
So you may wonder
Watching these two whom the train indifferently bears.[1]

There are at least two ways of travelling on this train. A third possibility is a different way of being, way of knowing, way of behaving. It involves living as if beneath the obverse side of a tapestry. You don't stride magisterially across the magic carpet as though you owned it and had an inalienable right to comprehend it; you don't claim to understand it by examining closely its exact measurement, its weight, its texture, its colour, its pattern, its density; rather you cling to its underside and examine as best you can the various threads that combine to make up the picture on top. This topside you will never be able to see as a panorama, but you can at least surmise what it might look like from imaginative guesswork based upon evidence available on the underside. The obverse danglings within your reach determine, in however threadbare a fashion, the splendour of the tapestry above. A tapestry is woven from different-coloured threads. Images and designs emerge from the interplay of colour and texture. Whereas the front of the tapestry might be a recognisable masterpiece, the back is a mess. What is clear on the front is opaque at the back. Where the front is smooth and coherent, the back is a chaos of knots and loose ends.

Corrie Ten Boom, a survivor of the concentration camps of World War II, expresses something of the same intuition quoting from the poem 'Life is but a Weaving' by Benjamin Malachi Franklin. When the Nazis invaded Holland, her quiet life was turned into a nightmare. She had made her home a 'hiding place' for Jews, and for so doing she and her family were punished. Her 84-year-old father died in the prison at Scheveningen near The Hague; Corrie and her sister Betsie were taken

---

1 C. Day Lewis, *The Complete Poems*, Sinclair Stevenson, London, 1992, p. 401, verses 1,3,5.

to Ravensbrück near Berlin where Betsie died on December 16th, 1944, five months before the war ended. Corrie survived and was someone – despite everything – who could analyse the mystery of existence and maintain faith in its meaning.

LIFE IS BUT A WEAVING
(the Tapestry Poem)

My life is but a weaving
Between my God and me.
I cannot choose the colours
He weaveth steadily.

Oft' times He weaveth sorrow;
And I in foolish pride
Forget He sees the upper
And I the underside.

Not 'til the loom is silent
And the shuttles cease to fly
Will God unroll the canvas
And reveal the reason why.

The dark threads are as needful
In the weaver's skillful hand
As the threads of gold and silver
In the pattern He has planned

He knows, He loves, He cares;
Nothing this truth can dim.
He gives the very best to those
Who leave the choice to Him.

This is the way she reads the underside of the tapestry. Such reading has its own laws and exigencies, as demanding as any other way we have been taught to read. It is not the way of the Yellow-Eyed Hawk which hovers above its terrain in masterful control of both its own comprehension and the detailed map stretched out in full exposure before it.

Undersiders are allowed only oblique access to the panorama of the obverse side. However, the mysterious particles which adorn the underside are always actual participants in the reality above, and each can become a pointer towards what happens to it when it emerges in the ensemble towards which it contributes. Because there is less, and less obvious, material to engage with, our imaginations are called towards more allusive conjecture. Language too has to adapt itself to the situation and be stretched to accommodate the, often, unpredictable leaps which intuition is required to make.

Essentially, however we approach it, our being is a mystery never to be fully understood. We never can eject ourselves from the spaceship so as to obtain an objective outside view of what we are. We are always irretrievably situated on the inside and can only hope to glimpse through portholes the vastness, the complexity and the intricacy of the reality to which we belong. Apart from this bewilderment, so many aspects of our lives fall outside the compass of our comprehension: illness, death, disaster; emotion, love, ecstasy; such 'things' we name, but if truth be told, we know not what they are. We speak the world we have been thrown into by giving names to 'this' and 'that,' which are the realities we see and hear, taste, touch and smell around us. Our language is secondary; it is our blundering way of putting words on a more primary and nameless revelation. Furthermore, if I want to share such flashes of insight with another person, I use whatever ingenuity of expression is available to me to make that other person aware of the inexpressible reality I am trying to communicate.

If I want to make myself understood by a Japanese and we know no common language, I will point to the sky, saying 'sky,' and ask him with a gesture what 'that' is called in his language. He understands me and says his word. *What* did he understand? *What* do we have in common? I point to *that*, the sky, and he understands that this *that* is the sky – not the air, not the blue, etc. We understood each other without words: he grasped which *that* I was pointing to and this that was already word, beyond any particular language. He grasped the *real* word, pure understanding, of which every sign, every spoken word, is only an indication. Such wordless understanding makes translation possible. It makes a thing a *thing*. This wordless word is not an outer 'name' attached to a thing, it *is* the thing.[2]

Two things become apparent from this juxtaposition: the world itself makes us speak; it provides the wherewithal of any dialogue. Earthly speech is not given to us with our physical birth; we learn it slowly and tediously. Our language is secondary; it is our blundering way of putting words on primary inarticulate experience revealed in and by the world we share. Pointing, indicating, grasping and wanting to grasp, are the first appearances of speech, and any definitive articulation of the mystery must always remain tentative and unsure, always ready for a more effective, understandable and communicable way of putting it. We share with one another what we have inherited, by pointing towards what we perceive, and agreeing upon sounds and vocabulary which best describe such realities.

Some of the words we use are clear because they are unambiguous and without mystery; through such words we acquire mastery over things, in the way we look up handbooks for gadgets we use every day. But the

<hr />

2   Georg Kühlewind, *Becoming Aware of the Logos, The Way of St John the Evangelist*, Lindisfarne Press, 1983, p. 16.

mysterious world I am trying to evoke requires another kind of word and vocabulary. Such words may seem obscure because they evoke the depths of the mystery, but such is their function, and they cannot allow themselves to betray the subtlety by aping clarity. They open a door to realities we had never imagined before and this requires whatever ingenuity must be galvanised to achieve this end. Such words, which often spring from the heart of poets, are original words, as opposed to the kind that clutter our landscape: jargon, propaganda, clichés. The power of the original word that really moves us is that it allows us to see differently the ordinary world in which we were living up to then.

Such an understanding provides an alternative dimension to daily existence. We understand that the world around us is the shop-front for a greater reality. And as an integral part of this world, like a figure in a doll's house, we too, each one of us, are more than we might be able to identify. Apart from the biological, chronological, geographically located identity that is you, who were born on a certain date, occupied a certain space on the planet and fulfilled a very specific and recorded curriculum vitae during your lifetime, until you die and are buried on another specific and identifiable date, there is a bigger 'you' which exceeds this meagre and quantifiable slice of existence. And so it is with every other particle of this universe, everything links in with a more expansive weave and web. We belong to a deeper root system which creates patterns and echoes from more distant horizons. What we may be experiencing today as one lonely horizontal thread emerging from the path in front of us, could reveal itself to be, in the multi-dimensional tapestry of human history, a harmonic note within a larger, deeper matrix.

Accustomed as we are to the anchored swivel range of the human viewpoint, we are tethered to short-sightedness. We have to imagine the alternative space and time which makes of every element within the created world, including ourselves, a meaningful part of a greater whole. Our biological life from birth to death is bankrolled by counterfeit currency unless we consciously switch to an alternative energy, a superior wattage, which allows us to surmise that we ourselves, and everything that exists in our world around us, are not simply self-contained things in themselves, but manifestations of a larger reality, signals from a vaster energy.

PART I

YELLOW-EYED HAWK OF THE MIND

This title is borrowed from W.B. Yeats. He uses it in a different context. I take it to describe our minds as they have been allowed to develop. For over three centuries now we have been trained like hawks. We have latched onto one particular aspect of consciousness and valorised it to the point of excluding all other kinds of intellectual investigation. A.N. Whitehead suggested that: 'the 17th Century had produced a scheme of scientific thought framed by mathematicians for the use of mathematicians.'[3] And we have bought into this schema and force-fed it to our children as the great privilege of organised education. It is as if we had been taught falconry in the 17th Century and had become so obsessed by this absorbing and accomplished sport that we neglect to the point of exclusion all the other birds in the aviary, more particularly, those of paradise. As a result, our culture admits only one world. This is measured by geometry (meaning in Greek, geo-metry 'measurement of the world') and counted in numbers containing no ambiguity. There is only one kind of space and time which are presented as absolute and invariant. There is no question of 'my' space or 'your' space, there is only an inventory of impersonal locations and dates: a map of the world for anthropologists anonymous.

Of course, there is an advantage to having such a common language. Science provides us with formulae which are supposed to mean the same thing to every human being no matter who or where you are. If you run 100 metres faster than your rival at the other side of the world, both you and your competitor have to agree about the exact distance you have run and the time in which you took to run it. Such measurements

---

3   A.N. Whitehead, *Science and the Modern World*, Freepress, p. 57.

are standardised. Thus, a world record in the 100 metres sprint can be recorded in any part of the world at any time and, if verified officially, must be accepted as fact by every one in every other part of the world. A metre used to be one ten-millionth part of a meridian that passes from the pole to the equator (reproduced in platinum on the official metre stick kept in Paris) until in October 1960 when it became universally accepted as 1,650,753.73 wavelengths of the orange-red light of krypton 86. A second is one three-thousandth-six-hundredth of a twenty-fourth part of a period of the Earth's rotation on its axis. Cold but also comforting: the language of science is invariant and universal. Even if you don't understand it, you accept it as standardised fact. The space we live in is an ordered totality of concrete extensions; the time, an ordered totality of concrete durations. It doesn't matter what anyone feels like, that's all subjective and personal. What we are looking for is an objective assessment: a picture of the world from nobody's point of view. If you arrive in a city you don't want a sentimentally biased account of what someone else thinks you should see, you want a map which will show you where you are, where you could go, and how you can get there no matter who you are or how you are feeling.

Science sees existence as reducible to a number of universal laws. It then makes interconnections between these. Everything has a reason, an explanation, a cause. Patient observation will reveal the cause and these causes interconnect to form a set of laws about the world we live in which offer a satisfactory explanation for all that is. We have a cultural bias in favour of this scientific way of understanding. And there is every reason for such inclination. Science has worked wonders at every level of our wellbeing.

But it is still necessary to know that science is not everything. As long as we recognise that we are steeped in a bias there is some hope of redressing the balance in favour of another kind of reality, impenetrable by such a mentality. I hope to describe another kind of knowing which can open horizons beyond the world of facts, events and measureable data.

The Yellow-Eyed Hawk has no time for dilly-dallying. All considerations outside the area being surveyed for booty and forage are a waste of time and energy needed for the fray. Full attention is required, without distraction, for the scientific purpose of fully comprehending the world we live in.

> I am monarch of all I survey
> My right there is none to dispute;
> From the centre all round to the sea
> I am lord of the fowl and the brute.[4]

Religion, for the Yellow-Eyed Hawk, is a distraction. It feeds us with fantasy and illusion; it is 'the opium of the people,' as Marx intimated, keeping people in their place; and, more disturbingly, causing much of the conflict on our planet. It is part of the mental baggage that should have been discarded long ago, especially since we came of age as rational animals. Mental hygiene requires its removal from our desk-tops, so that we can get on with the realistic business of negotiating our limited span of time on this miniscule world of ours, without deception or delusion.

The purpose of this book is to suggest otherwise. Not that I am trying in any way to denigrate or discount the undeniable benefits, the unbelievable improvements and discoveries of the Yellow-Eyed Hawk. How could anybody living in the 21st Century fail to applaud? But are there not more things in Heaven and on Earth, Oh Hawk-Eye, "than are dreamt of in your philosophy"?[5] Beyond the range and vision of the Yellow-Eyed Hawk could there not be other realities impervious to its gaze? Mathematics and physics, by the nature of their operative efficacy, dissociate from the subjective world of feeling. This leaves out a vital dimension that holds that "inhabited space transcends geometrical

---

4   William Cowper, 'The Solitude of Alexander Selkirk'.
5   Cf. William Shakespeare, *Hamlet*, Act 1, Scene 5, 167-8.

space".[6] My garden may be 100 metres long but every inch of it possesses more reality than can ever be recorded by a measuring stick. Every centimetre from the place we occupy with our bodies is alive with reality unaccounted for by objective topography. The tiny creatures the hawk espies as prey have underground burrows into which they can scuttle to enter a world that is barred to the hawk. Music, art, myth, for instance, are symbolic systems that allow us to process the subtle way in which the world attaches itself to our sensibility and our psyches.

6   Gaston Bachelard, *The Poetics of Space*, Penguin Books, New York, 2014, p. 54.

TRAINING THE HAWK

In a short story called 'William and Mary', Roald Dahl describes how Mary Pearl's husband William has passed away one week ago, and after the lawyer reads the will, he gives her a letter from her dead husband. She returns home to read it. She is shocked to discover 20 pages describing a scientific experiment for which an Oxford colleague had convinced him to volunteer. After his death from cancer, William's brain was hooked up to an artificial heart machine and removed from his skull. It now resides in a basin of cerebrospinal fluid and only exists because the machines keep pumping it full of oxygenated blood. The doctor, Landy, has even managed to save one of William's eyes, which is connected to his brain by the optic nerve and which now floats on top of the fluid in a plastic case. William urges Mary to put aside her revulsion and come to visit him and see how the experiment turned out.

In something of a similar experiment, we have managed to develop the very topmost part of our brains in an autonomous and almost complete disconnect from the rest of our bodies and from the totality of our personalities. This has happened over a very long period of cultural confinement and educational endeavour but has been accelerated in even more concentrated doses over the last four centuries.

Civilised societies of the 20th Century democratised the languages of reading, writing and arithmetic – the so-called three 'Rs'. These became fundamental educational currency. They also became criteria for judging 'intelligence' measured by narrow tests of IQ. The development of the three Rs as the standard syllabus for all primary education lost us our capacity to see life as mystery and prepared us to face it as problems to be solved.

People of Western Europe in the 20th Century were not only able to read and write more or less instinctively, they translated everything that presented itself to them into this narrow framework. We imagine that reading and writing are natural to us, whereas, in fact, they must be two of the most unnatural activities undertaken by any animal. And yet, because of our educational endeavours, reading and writing have become for most of us as 'natural' as walking and talking. We have been trained to receive the world sequentially and in fragmented slices which are delivered to our brains through written characters on a page. This second-hand translation of reality into cut and dried black and white print has become so normal to us that we reduce all our immediate sensation of the world around us to this particular myopic funnel. We read our lives and leave out whatever cannot be translated into this medium. It is as if we were snorting reality like a powdered line of cocaine through the tiny filter of a single nostril.

People also have to learn to read and write the language of measurement, if they are to understand modern science. This means a no-nonsense approach to numbers which are deprived of any potential magic.

Walter Ong has examined the history of our versatility in these areas and has explained how and why our language abilities got cut off from our instinctive vernacular and thereby from our unconscious some centuries back. He shows how a language such as Latin, which was once spoken by the Romans as an indigenous dialect, had later become the *lingua franca* of an empire, until eventually it turned into a dead language, killing something vital in those forced to use it.

'High Latin' which was never a 'mother tongue' (taught by one's mother) to later generations of Europeans, became their only access to Higher Education. Once a spoken language it turned into a 'school language,' completely controlled by writing, and it ceased to be a vernacular tongue for those who used it.

For well over 1,000 years Latin was a language written and spoken by males, for the most part. It was nobody's mother tongue and was learnt outside the home as a foreign language. It had no direct connection with the unconscious as any vernacular learnt from early childhood would have. There was no baby-talk associated with it and it was taught with all the punitive hardships and rigorous academic settings which were the hallmarks of our schools. It was a first language to none of its users and since each of them spoke it with an accent peculiar to their particular country, none of them could understand it as spoken by the other. This meant that it became essentially a written language because it was always recorded in the same way and could be understood as a written text by all who had learnt it.

This 'learned Latin' became a striking example of how the power of writing first of all isolates discourse. It has to be translated into an objective form before it can become part of a dialogue. But this very isolation was also the cause of an unparalleled productivity, which was the result of such concentrated solitude. This strange phenomenon made possible "the exquisitely abstract world of medieval scholasticism" which in turn created the "the new mathematical modern science which followed on the scholastic experience".[7] Ong suggests that without Learned Latin as an abstract written language cut off from the psychic roots of our normal vernacular languages, "modern science would have got under way with greater difficulty, if it had got under way at all". Our kind of literacy and numeracy is rooted in the abstract written language, which was the *lingua franca* of all the universities of Europe for 1,000 years. "Modern science grew in Latin soil," according to Ong, "for philosophers and scientists through the time of Sir Isaac Newton commonly both wrote and did their abstract thinking in Latin."

We are all victims or beneficiaries of this legacy depending on how you wish to view it. The results are spectacular in one way and can be proved immediately. What is happening at this moment for you as a reader is a case in point. Between you and me at this moment in your life, is a page

....

7   Walter J. Ong, *Orality and Literacy, The Technologising of the Word*, Routledge, London & New York, 1982, the edition I quote from is 2000, pp. 113-4.

of print. These words form a code which, because you can read and I can write, allow me to communicate with you. The process is similar to drip-feeding. A vast multitude crowds towards one tiny entrance where one word appears at a time. I can only write one word at a time. I fill this page slowly and separately so that I can tell you word for word what is on my mind. You have become so used to gobbling up these units that you may not even notice the cumbersome technique necessary for you to eventually land these ideas in your mind. The further complication is this: because we have now been taught to read almost automatically we tend to 'read' everything. This very complex skill which we have acquired has warped our sensibility. We have turned ourselves into text maniacs, we 'read' our lives. So, we have to ask ourselves whether we may not have lost almost as much as we have gained from our much-vaunted literacy and numeracy skills.

The problem with our inherited world is not the hierarchy of different symbolic systems which are available to us to enjoy the spectrum of experience which spans the radar screen of human consciousness, it is, rather, the dearth of such systems when it comes to neglected areas, especially those which are unconscious. We have only to think of the language of emotion to find an area where education and trained sensibility are in short supply.

Each person is left to fend for themselves in one of the most poignant and inescapable areas of our experience. And yet it seems obvious that each of us should be given at least the rudiments of one of the most elusive and important symbolic systems if we are to begin to understand human relationships. This would require tapping into a wavelength and a communications system other than the cerebral. Reaching what has been called the 'sympathetic system' as opposed to the cerebrospinal one which covers the three Rs of traditional education.

There is a language of symbols which can help us to grapple with the unconscious. But we neglect it and automatically revert to what we have been taught at school. We *read* music, art, cinema, life and love. Every time we enter an art gallery how many of us don't look at the pictures but read the little label posted at the side. Faced by an abstract painting of white on white we are totally bemused until we read the caption at the side which says: 'aeroplane gone out of sight'. Now we understand. Everything we do must be a story, an alphabet, a grammar, a plot, a chapter, a closed book, a best seller. We read and write our lives and we have bought into this scheme of things to the extent that we are allowing it to be force-fed to our children in the name of 'free education'.

From four years old we have been subjected, and our children are being subjected, to a bookish, commercial education. Compulsory education in our world came into being not more than 200 years ago. Charles Dickens who was born on February 7th, 1812, and died on June 9th, 1870, lived around the same time. He was aware from the very beginning that this educational experiment was headed in the wrong direction. His novel *Hard Times*, published in 1852, provides a colourful caricature. The first three chapters describe Mr Gradgrind, whose name even suggests a cram school, laying out his educational philosophy. Chapter One is called 'The One Thing Needful' and Mr Gradgrind extrapolates in the opening salvo:

'Now, what I want is Facts. Teach these boys and girls nothing but Facts. Facts alone are wanted in life. Plant nothing else, and root out everything else. You can only form the minds of reasoning animals upon Facts; nothing else will ever be of any service to them.'

In Chapter Two, called 'Murdering the Innocents,' we meet 'Mr M'Choakumchild,' who with "some 140 other schoolmasters, had been lately turned at the same time, in the same factory, on the same principles, like so many pianoforte legs". His job is to teach facts to the "vessels ranged before him" and to root out fancy. "You mustn't fancy. That's it! You are never to fancy."

Chapter Three, called 'A loophole,' introduces a three-ringed circus as the epitome of fancy. Mr Gradgrind, walking home very pleased with himself and with the education he is providing for his five children, congratulates himself that:

> no little Gradgrind had ever seen a face in the moon . . . No little Gradgrind had ever learnt the silly jingle, Twinkle, twinkle, little star! No little Gradgrind had ever associated a cow in a field with that famous cow who jumped over the moon, . . . and had only been introduced to a cow as 'a gramnivorous ruminating quadruped with several stomachs'. But, *horribile dictu*, reaching the horse-riding establishment belonging to the circus
> . . . what did he then behold but his own metallurgical Louisa, peeping with all her might through a hole in a deal board, and his own mathematical Thomas abasing himself on the ground to catch but a hoof of the graceful equestrian Tyrolean flower-act!
> Dumb with amazement, Mr Gradgrind crossed to the spot where his family was thus disgraced, laid his hand upon each erring child, and said:
> 'Louisa!! Thomas!!'
> Both rose, red and disconcerted.
> 'In the name of wonder, idleness, and folly!' said Mr Gradgrind, leading each away by a hand; 'what do you do here?'
> 'Wanted to see what it was like,' returned Louisa, shortly.
> There was an air of jaded sullenness in them both, and particularly in the girl: yet, struggling through the dissatisfaction of her face, there was a light with nothing to rest upon, a fire with nothing to burn, a starved imagination keeping life in itself somehow, which brightened its expression. Not with the brightness natural to cheerful youth, but with uncertain, eager, doubtful flashes, which had something painful in them, analogous to the changes on a blind face groping its way.

Ours is the dilemma of the Gradgrind children. We have been educated out of the circus ring, the realm of fancy. The only world-view we know is the one prescribed by the Department of Education. Apart from this 'world' there is no other. And we are tired of this world. It may be the only 'logical' one, the only one offering the security of a pensionable job and coherent structure, but it does not answer to the deep yearnings of our souls. In a later chapter of *Hard Times*, Louisa says to her father:

> You have been so careful of me that I never had a child's heart. You have trained me so well that I never dreamed a child's dream. You have dealt so wisely with me, Father, from my cradle to this hour, that I never had a child's belief or a child's fear.

Far from being taken aback or disconcerted, "Mr Gradgrind is moved by his success, and by this testimony to it. 'My dear Louisa,' said he, 'you abundantly repay my care. Kiss me, my dear girl.'"

Kathleen Raine, who was born in 1908 and who died at the age of 95 in the year 2003, summed up herself and the century through which she had lived:

> A child of my time, who at Cambridge read Natural Sciences, and rejected my Christian heritage in order to adopt with uncritical zeal the current scientific orthodoxy of that university, I have lived long enough to come full circle. It is all that I learned in my Cambridge days that I have little by little come to reject . . . A slow learner, I have been blessed with a long life which has brought me back to a knowledge not taught in our schools. [8]

Most of our education from the age of four is at a third remove from the reality which we perceive around us. Between the metric space of

8   Kathleen Raine, *W.B. Yeats and the Learning of the Imagination*, Golgonooza Press, 1999, pp. 5-6.

mathematics and physics and the topological space of our childhood world there are several symbolic variations to which we have access as children and which we ignore and abandon to our cost. Children are naturally in touch with all parts of their brains, but such capabilities seem to have been erased by the age of 18.

> Before he went to school
> he could read
> the barks of trees,
> leaf veins,
> footprints,
> and the touch of fingers;
> now he goes to school,
> and he can only read words.
>
> *Jennifer Farley*

William Butler Yeats certainly believed in knowledge of another kind. Here is his introduction to Lady Gregory's *Gods and Fighting Men* (1904): "Children play at being great and wonderful people," at the ambitions they will put away for one reason or another before they grow into ordinary men and women. "Mankind as a whole had a like dream once; everybody and nobody built up the dream bit by bit and the story-tellers are there to make us remember."

Listen to John Carey, professor of literature in Oxford, reviewing, some years ago, Roy Foster's biography of Yeats: "Was he, you find yourself blasphemously wondering, really that intelligent?" and Carey lists the usual proofs of intellectual backwardness: "He was substandard at school . . . He never learnt to spell: even as a grown man, simple monosyllables foxed him . . . His gullibility was fathomless. Mysticism and magic, to which he was introduced by the half-batty George Russell, occupied much of his waking and sleeping life. He believed he conversed with old Celtic gods and a copious ragbag of other supernaturals."[9]

We have to get over the laughter. Yeats' intelligence was essentially mythic. "I wished for a world where I could discover this tradition perpetually, and not in pictures and in poems only, but in tiles round the chimney-piece and in the hangings that kept out the draught. I had even created a dogma: Because those imaginary people are created out of the deepest instinct of man, to be his measure and his norm, whatever I can imagine those mouths speaking may be the nearest I can go to truth."[10]

Even to understand this last quotation we have to reintroduce ourselves to a mythic way of thinking. Such intelligence weaves its way through symbols and has a very different perspective on the universe to that of the scientist. Richard Dawkins carries the following quote from John Carey on his website and introduces it as follows:

> Could science just be too difficult for some people, and therefore seem threatening? Oddly enough, I wouldn't dare to make such a suggestion, but I am happy to quote a distinguished literary scholar, John Carey, the present Merton Professor of English at Oxford: "The annual hordes competing for places on arts courses in British universities, and the trickle of science applicants, testify to the abandonment of science among the young. Though most academics are wary of saying it straight out, the general consensus seems to be that arts courses are popular because they are easier, and that most arts students would simply not be up to the intellectual demands of a science course."[11]

Here science and the scientific way of thinking are regarded as the norm and other ways of thinking are measured against these and found

9   John Carey, 'Poetic License', The Sunday Times, 9 March 1997, sec. 8, p. 1.

10 William Butler Yeats, *Four Years 1887-1891*, The Cuala Press, Dublin, 1921, pp. 4-5, later published in Autobiographies, op. cit. pp. 115-116.

11 *www.edge.org/3rd_culture/dawkins/lecture_p6.html.*

wanting. However, this is to overlook the possibility that there are other ways of knowing which are quite different from those emphasised and promoted to the exclusion of all others by our recent culture.

Mythic intelligence weaves its way through symbols and has a very different perspective on the universe to that of the scientist. A poem may be "the residue of . . . the ghost within every experience that wishes it could be seen or felt, acknowledged as a kind of meaning . . . A poem is a place where the conditions of beyondness and withinness are made palpable."[12] As Peter Kingsley writes in his book *Reality*:

> Once the direction . . . was still known about. But that was a long time ago. And now there is no way you could even start to discover it again through reasoning, because reasoning is precisely what covered it over in the first place; is what did everything possible to obliterate its traces. The only way to find it is through your neglected sense of smell . . . [not] smell that used to tell where your territory begins and someone else's ends, but about something even more instinctive: the scent of recognition, of rediscovering ancient links and affinities long forgotten . . . And with this recognition comes sweetness – along with the knowledge that things will be simpler now. The hardest part is already over. The greatest struggle is behind us, and what lies ahead is like the joy of opening your mouth to rain or of running effortlessly down a gentle grassy slope.[13]

We have borrowed our education systems from armies, conquerors, mathematicians, scientists and technologists. These should provide only

12 *The Making of a Poem*, A Norton Anthology of Poetic Forms, edited by Mark Strand and Eavan Boland, New York, Norton, 2000, p. xxix.
13 Peter Kingsley, *Reality*, The Golden Sufi Center, California, 2003, p. 317.

one half of what education might mean. The industrial revolution, the scientific revolution, the technological revolution, the cybernetic revolution: all these have transformed our lives and we are grateful to them. We know also that they need young hands to keep them going, to make them work, to maintain the infrastructure of our Western World. But these very important realities with which our education system is obsessed, have been allowed to crowd out the tiny flowers of imagination. There must be more to life than science. That 'more' is an inner garden of the imagination that each of us should be allowed to cultivate, where we should be encouraged to dwell for at least some part of our days and lives.

HAWKING THE TRADITION

Since the end of the 19th Century and the beginning of the 20th Century, most religious thought systems waged war against science as an ungodly and irreligious attempt to hijack the planet for atheistic purposes. In their turn, most self-respecting scientists of the same period had to be agnostic and positivist. Religion was regarded as superstition, for which scientific explanation could be provided in terms of 'compensation', 'projection', 'opium of the people'.

When religion was summoned to the courtroom of the Yellow-Eyed Hawk and asked to give an account of itself, the odds were stacked against it. An idiom quite foreign to religious sensibility was the recognised process of investigation. 'What kind of scientific verification can you provide for the incredible realities you require your adherents to accept?'

Instead of rejecting out of hand the question as posed and the process involved; instead of explaining that an alternative language and methodology are required to approach the topics being investigated; too many Church authorities insisted on trying to defend, on scientific grounds, the basis for their religious beliefs. Our 'scientific' culture has trained our minds to work on what Paul Ricoeur has named "a hermeneutics of suspicion," which automatically precludes any system of belief. Rita Felski describes the hermeneutics of suspicion as "a commitment to unmasking the lies and illusions of consciousness;" those who employ it "are the architects of a distinctively modern style of interpretation that circumvents obvious or self-evident meanings in order to draw out less visible and less flattering truths;" and their methodology is a "technique of reading texts against the grain and between the lines, of cataloguing their omissions and laying bare their contradictions, of rubbing in what they fail to know and cannot represent".[14] In such an atmosphere, attempts to introduce a world other than the one we see verifiably before us are laughed out of court.

Those defending religion should not begin by drawing up scientific proof for what is, of its essence, unprovable. Religion requires, rather, a hermeneutics of positive conjecture, a willingness to suspend disbelief. To connect with the sacred we need to affirm what we cannot see, even when and if our intellects, as they are presently honed, are unwilling and unable to do this. "Negative capability," the phrase coined by Keats, is possibly the best way to describe the capacity to pursue a vision even when it leads to intellectual confusion and uncertainty. Keats uses the phrase to describe artists, especially Shakespeare, who are "capable of being in uncertainties, mysteries, doubts, without any irritable reaching after fact and reason".[15] The term can also be used in a more general way to describe the ability of the individual to perceive, think, and operate beyond any presupposition of a predetermined nature. It suggests a more magnanimous and open-minded approach to possibilities in the reality around us and trusts the capacity of the human being to think beyond the narrow confines laid down by arbitrary philosophies and preconceived systems. "I compare human life to a large Mansion of Many Apartments, two of which I can only describe, the doors of the rest being as yet shut upon me . . . We are in a Mist—We are now in that state—We feel the 'burden of the Mystery'."[16]

We must call on more than a purely intellectual life to connect with a world beyond this one. But having begun the battle on the wrong foot, religions have sometimes refused to change their stance and have continued to defend the scientifically indefensible. We must surely have

14 Rita Felson, 'Critique and the Hermeneutics of Suspicion', *Journal of Media and Culture*, Vol 15, no. 1, 2012.
15 John Keats (1899), *The Complete Poetical Works and Letters of John Keats*, Cambridge Edition, Houghton, Mifflin and Company, p. 277.
16 Ibid. p. 326.

learnt over the last century that attempts to support religion through scientifically provable evidence, or even, by obsequious and supposedly conciliatory back pedalling, to avoid conflict with science, simply do not work. An example of this is the ongoing battle between so-called creationists and evolutionists, which can be summarised in the simplified conundrum: Did life on Earth evolve over millions of years, or was it created in the blink of an eye by God?

Creationism is mostly a Judaeo-Christian stand-point, being based upon a literal reading of the Bible which describes the creation of the world and all of life over a period of six days. Advances in geology in the 1700s and 1800s, and especially Charles Darwin's *The Origin of Species*, published in 1859, shook the foundations of any such literal belief. Instead of admitting that the Book of Genesis, like so many other archaic texts, was written in a poetic mode with purposes other than scientific in mind, biblical fundamentalists dug in their heels and tried to defend the scientific accuracy of every word of the sacred text.

20th Century engagement in such battles finds a stereotype in the 1925 Scopes Monkey Trial. Tennessee schoolteacher John Scopes incriminated himself for teaching evolution in a classroom, deliberately flouting a state law. Clarence Darrow defended Scopes while three-time presidential candidate Williams Jennings Bryan prosecuted. All America listened on radio. Scopes was found guilty and fined $100. The Tennessee Supreme Court later overturned the verdict on a technicality, but upheld the law preventing evolution from being taught. The debate continues to this day.

The difference now is that most scientists hold that evolution is a well-established scientific theory that explains the origins and development of life on Earth. Scientific theory, they tell us, is not guesswork but an established explanation for a natural phenomenon, repeatedly tested through observation and experimentation. Indeed, most scientists argue that, for all practical purposes, evolution through natural selection is a fact. Creation is dismissed.

The popular media often portrays the creation vs. evolution debate as science vs. religion. You can find yourself condemned and 'exposed' as a religious fanatic, trying to redeem a ridiculous, prescientific, religious worldview. On the other hand, more recent scepticism finds so many gaps in knowledge and leaps in conjecture attached to the theory of evolution, that it becomes as much a matter of 'faith' for its adherents as creationism is for its followers.

By the middle of the last century, in the 1950s, most thinking people had become aware that far from being created about 10,000 years ago, our Earth was about 4,550 million years old (plus or minus a few 70 million years). Shame and amazement that we took so long to understand the planet on which we had been intelligently standing for over 26 centuries suggested a conspiracy between Church and State to prevent us from seeing what was directly in front of us, providing simplistic alternatives backed by authoritative guarantees.

The heliocentric theory of Copernicus, for instance, had a profound and negative impact on official religion. Copernicus himself was careful during his life not to incur ecclesiastical wrath. For fear of censure, he delayed publication of his findings. He even dedicated, with apparent sincerity, the famous work in which he proclaims his heliocentric theory to the Pope of the day. Only later, in Galileo's time, did the Church condemn Copernicus' work also. Galileo was summoned to Rome to stand trial on suspicion of heresy "for holding as true the false doctrine taught by some that the sun is the centre of the world". In 1616 the Holy Office condemned Galileo's Copernican teaching as "foolish, preposterous and heretical, because contrary to Scripture". Before the cardinals and inquisitors, the old man was forced to recite, while kneeling, "I abjure, curse and detest the aforesaid errors and heresies". He was originally to be imprisoned, however due to his advanced age (70 at the time of the trial), the sentence was later commuted to house arrest for the remainder of his life. His offending *Dialogue* was banned and publication of any of his works was forbidden, including any he might write in the future.

It was not until 1758 that the Catholic Church dropped the general prohibition of texts advocating heliocentrism from the Index of Forbidden Books. It did not, however, explicitly rescind the decisions issued by the Inquisition in its judgement against Galileo, nor did it lift the prohibition of publication of uncensored versions of Copernicus's *De Revolutionibus*.

Almost to add insult to injury, in the year 2000, Pope John Paul II issued a formal apology for all the mistakes committed over the previous 2,000 years of the Catholic Church's history, including the trial of Galileo.

It was not only the Roman Catholic Church, armed with the back-up of the Inquisition, who defended such theories, condemning proposed alternatives based on scientific observation. Archbishop Ussher (1581–1656), Church of Ireland Archbishop of Armagh and Primate of All Ireland, famously proved that the creation of the world took place on the night preceding October 23rd, 4004BC.

Our difficulty here is that we are trying to translate one idiom into another. We are asking myth to stand and deliver, to identify itself in the court of scientific reason. If our culture insists that only historical events have validity, only what can be empirically verified has truth, we are in a dilemma. We have to admit that trying to squeeze the mysteries of Christianity, or any other religion, into the straitjacket of science was a mistake, not because these mysteries are false but because they speak an alternative language. As Kevin Treston puts it: "Christianity urgently needs to recover an appreciation of the world of *mythos* if it is going to communicate the Gospel effectively. The prospects are bleak if it operates out of a literalist mode within a scientific cultural environment."[17] Religious myth cannot be grasped intellectually. Imagination has to supply what the rational mind is unable to provide, beginning with respect for symbols as justifiable and proficient vehicles of a certain

....

17 Quoted in David Tacey, *Religion as Metaphor, Beyond Literal Belief,* Transaction Publishers, New Brunswick, 2015, p. 213.

kind of truth. We cannot allow spiritual truth to be placed in the same category as fantasy, or fiction. Mythic truth must survive its banishment from the realms of validity at the hands of scientific imperialism. Instead of holding that religious teachings about creation and scientific theories of evolution need not contradict each other, religious leaders insisted on staunchly defending teachings which had lost all credibility.

Mythology is a genre of its own which corresponds to a very ancient structural fabric of our human minds and hearts. Myths deal with mystery. As most of our lives are embedded in puzzlement quite beyond our ken, such a bedazzled section of our epistemological makeup is a much-underrated faculty. Mythic intelligence has its own language which indeed borrows from a more standard alphabet and vocabulary but it then leaves traces of itself on our more limited human mindscape. Mythological mystery-speak provides a doorway to another kind of consciousness leading us, not towards scientifically established facts of history, but towards truths in another dimension.

Neither myth nor mystery can ever fully be understood by our customary human reasoning which was not designed to encompass them. They introduce us to realities which we can never fully understand, and they present these in language which allows us to imagine something beyond our reach intellectually. For the most part we are a mystery to ourselves. We live our lives in a small area of artificial light which we call consciousness. We choose to live and move in our day-to-day world within this orbit. Once we find ourselves outside it, or when intimations from outside filter in, we are tongue-tied. We search for a language to communicate with the magical, the mysterious, the impenetrable. This should make us aware that there is a vast area beyond our normal day-to-day comprehension which we have learned to call the unconscious, simply because we have no idea about it. We were not always aware of it, and only comparatively recently have we recognised how important it is. Not only do we have to acknowledge its existence but we should also try to integrate it as much as possible into the way we run our lives. It is now over a century since we rediscovered this reality about ourselves and yet, we have to admit, our ways of conducting our lives and our systems of education have hardly changed at all to try to accommodate such a vast reality.

There are a number of ways to gain access to the unconscious. The first is by being attentive to our dreams. We dream every night but we may not be conscious of it. It takes time and attention to let ourselves become aware of such dreams. They are the language of our unconscious telling us what we refuse to tell ourselves during our daylight hours. Nor are they easy to interpret. We have to learn to crack the code. We have to find out about the shadow side of ourselves. This is not a luxury, an optional extra. It has become mandatory. One of the major obstacles to dealing with this reality in an effective way is the refusal to admit that it exists at all, or the conviction that it is unnecessary to engage with it and try to integrate it into our psychological, our social and our educated selves.

Apart from our own dreamtime, there is also the great reminder of this reality contained in the stories of our ancestors. What dreams are to individuals, myths and legends are to peoples. Such a storehouse exists for all of us as peoples of the Western world. Apart from the language of dreams and the storehouse of mythology there is the phenomenon of art.[18] Most great art issues from the unconscious.

....

18 I have approached the unconscious in terms of art in three previous books: *Kissing the Dark*, Veritas, Dublin, 1999; *The Haunted Inkwell*, Columba, Dublin, 2001; and *Anchoring the Altar*, Veritas, Dublin, 2002.

PART II

PART II

MYTH AS MORE THAN MEETS THE EYE

I suppose my appreciation of myth must come from not having been to school myself until I was nine years old. This allowed me time to experience the world as a child in the way a child naturally relates to it. Imagination is at its ripest in the first decade of our lives and is only because we are schooled to avoid it that our attention is turned in another direction. Left to themselves, children engage with the world as a magic realm where anything is possible. Play is their medium of connection. Everything is grist to the mill; nothing is impossible. The world is my oyster and everywhere hides a pearl. Adults are afraid of this capacity. It could so easily lead to megalomania, useless daydreaming and illusionary fantasy. As soon as possible they try to stop this nonsense, get us grounded in reality, acquainted with the hard facts of life. As a result, most people educated in the 20th Century are blind and deaf to mythology or symbolism, whether these are expressed in writing, in ritual, in 'divine beauty' as present in nature, or in the many-splendored language of art. Western European civilisation has long ago swapped this aspect of its birth right for a more productive mentality.

To offset such myopia, we must re-educate a world become blind and deaf to symbolism. Our mentor could be that inspired teacher, Anne Sullivan who taught Hellen Keller, born blind, deaf and mute, to retrieve her sensibility, her full humanity, her personality, her spirituality.

Let me remind you of the story. Anne arrived at the house in Tuscumbia, Alabama, to meet Helen Keller. After a month of Anne's teaching, what the people of the time called a 'miracle' occurred. Helen had until then never fully understood the meaning of words. When Anne led her to the water pump on April 5th, 1887 all that was about to change. Anne pumped the water over one of Helen's hands. She finger-spelled the word water in Helen's other hand. Something happened and the meaning of words became clear to Helen. Anne could immediately see in her face that Helen had finally understood. Helen recounted the incident in the autobiography she later was able to write: "We walked down the path to the well-house, attracted by the fragrance of the honey-suckle with which it was covered. Someone was drawing water and my teacher placed my hand under the spout. As the cool stream gushed over one hand she spelled into the other the word water, first slowly, then rapidly. I stood still, my whole attention fixed upon the motions of her fingers. Suddenly I felt a misty consciousness as of something forgotten, a thrill of returning thought, and somehow the mystery of language was revealed to me."

The kind of understanding which blind, deaf and mute, Helen Keller received at the water pump, whereby she began to understand the meaning of words, can be transposed to explain another kind of initiation to the world of myth. In such a context water, for instance, ceases to be merely the chemical formula H_2O, or as defined in the *Oxford Dictionary*, "a colourless, transparent, odourless, liquid". Another 'truth' about water emerges: that "it is an intrinsic part of most spiritual beliefs; that its uses and symbolism in religion are many and varied; that its spiritual and healing properties are seen in rites and rituals; and that its representations are as numerous as they are diverse. These different religious and cultural aspects of water reflect the vast array of civilizations that have made water the central element in their practices." (Courtesy of UNESCO Water and World Views).

Mythic intelligence is not something childish to be discarded as we grow up; it is an essential part of human understanding. The language of myth is specific; it carries a particular truth of its own. Between the perfect circles, squares, and oblongs which the architect placed on the table as the design of my garden there is another reality which we all know and recognise: my garden itself as I stroll through it in the morning, seeing the colours, hearing the birds and smelling the flowers; but then there is the Garden of Eden, for instance. All three are different realities, requiring three different kinds of understanding, three different usages of my knowing self. In the first case, the architect and I discuss abstract design, which requires geometrical and mathematical expression and precision; in the second I allow my senses to do the work of understanding as I look with my eyes, hear with my ears and smell with my nose. The Garden of Eden, on the other hand, brings into play my mythic intelligence.

For this, language has a different logic from the one we are used to in our everyday world. It is 'the forgotten language,' which became the title of a book by Eric Fromm. In this arena, space and time are no longer the ruling categories; intensity and association have as much right of way. "It is the one universal language the human race has ever developed; the same for all cultures and throughout history. It is a language with its own grammar and syntax ... a language one must understand if one is to understand the meaning of myths, fairy tales and dreams."[19]

Language was there before us and language encircled and invaded us long before we were ever conscious of it or of anything else. And so language itself, as it makes its way through us and uses our various faculties of self-expression, is a more fundamental expression of truth than the rational constructs that we might later invent for ourselves with our educated and cultivated mind-sets. Suddenly we recognise that there are utterances that occur from our childhood and from our interiority that by-pass the normal channels of our highly regulated and scrutinised conversation. These more primitive and less tutored utterances can be more authentic and more full-blooded manifestations of 'truth'. Poetry becomes the natural idiom of such pre-conceptual truth.

Ernst Cassirer in his study of *The Philosophy of Symbolic Forms*[20] explains how "the mythical intuition of space" occupies "a kind of middle position between the space of sense perception and the space of pure

---

19 Eric Fromm, *The Forgotten Language, An Introduction to the Understanding of Dreams, Fairy Tales and Myths*, Grove Press, New York, 1957, p. 7.

20 Ernst Cassirer, *The Philosophy of Symbolic Forms*, Yale University Press, 1955. *Volume I: Language; Volume 2: Mythical Thought; Volume 3: The Phenomenology of Knowledge; Volume 4: The Metaphysics of Symbolic Forms.*

cognition, that is, geometry". In fact, mathematical or geometrical, call it 'metric' space, cannot be derived from sensory space "in an unbroken logical sequence". The space of perception, which is the space of vision, of touch, of smell, of taste, of hearing, is not the same as the space of pure mathematics.

In sensory space and in mythical space there is no such thing as 'here' and 'there' as terms in a general or universal relation. Before-behind, above-below, right-left, are all completely different, what is called 'anisotropic'. What Casirer demonstrates is that "mythical space" is closely related to the space of sensory perception and further away from the logical space of geometry. In the first two every point and every element has a tonality of its own and a "special distinguishing character" which cannot be described in general concepts but must be immediately experienced as it is, for what it is. "In contrast to the homogeneity which prevails in the conceptual space of geometry every position and direction in mythical space is endowed as it were with a particular accent."[21]

Between me in the kitchen with the architect and me in the garden with all my senses ablaze, there is a middle posture that is 'mythic understanding'. This form of consciousness, this kind of knowledge, has every right to exist, to be cultivated, promoted, and valorised, just as much as the mathematical and geometrical.

Mircea Eliade reminds us that 'Mythos' is not "a stage in the history of consciousness," it is "a content in the structure of consciousness".[22] The language of myth is "indigenous" to the psyche, says David Tacey, and no amount of modernisation will get rid of it. It is how the psyche speaks.[23]

There is a language of symbols which can help us to grapple with the unconscious. The middle ages were fluent in such dialect. We, mostly because of the educational systems we have put in place, no longer see the

21 Ibid. *Volume 2*, pp. 83- 85.
22 Mircea Eliade, *The Quest: History and Meaning in Religion*, University of Chicago Press, Chicago, 1975, p. i.
23 David Tacey, *Religion as Metaphor*, Transaction Publishers, New Brunswick, 2015, p. 55.

world as symbols. Our world, like the island of Shakespeare's *Tempest*, is a confusion of bewildering lights and sounds to Caliban, but to Prospero it is the source of "clear signals from a different order of experience". We have to decide for ourselves, therefore, whether "to turn tail on it all like howling Caliban or to develop new powers of attention and perception capable of orchestrating this mad music".[24] The so-called 'mad music' of the 'sights and sounds' on our planet are directed towards a specific discernment centre in our understanding. They require the attention of our 'mytho-poetic' intelligence. Such a compound adjective is ugly and off-putting, and if you can think of a simpler and more direct way of saying it so much the better. For the moment it will have to do as a sobriquet or pseudonym for the reality being salvaged in these pages.

Anyone writing about divine realities, in the first century of the Christian era, would have used myth as their normal procedure, their preferred idiom. Ancient literature, and the Gospels cannot be excluded from this category, strove to depict in myths and dramas, not the day-to-day realities of anybody's life, but the eternal norms everywhere present in all life experience, the underlying structural grooves of created reality. Historical reporting, as we would understand it, was not regarded as appropriate for such sacred narratives. Journalistic reporting of eye-witnessed events could never be revelatory or even interesting. What the evangelists were recording were not ordinary everyday happenings. Their targets were signs and portents of something much larger: manifestations of the *Mirabilia Dei*, the wonderful workings of God in our world, which had happened before and would happen again, as it was in the beginning, is now, and ever shall be, world without end. Understanding such events and recording them accurately required more than a dictionary of ordinary language. The appointed scribe had to have recourse to the venerable wardrobe where all such materials from the past were stored. They had to rummage around for suitable and cannily appropriate resonances with

....
24 Alan McGlashan, *Savage and Beautiful Country*, Hillstone, New York, 1966.

which to deck out the happening they saw before them. These would help to connect the event with hidden lessons from the past, and associate it with other well-known and much loved interventions throughout history. The evangelists never intended to produce a bland eye-witness account of one particular person's life and times. They had a sacred story to tell which could only be recounted through metaphor and myth. In such an idiom this writing could also be a source of inspiration for all time, not simply an historical incident captured for a local audience.

We, in our culture, encounter this language as foreign or antiquated, something belonging to early childhood, which we should have left behind as we became adults. We are prepared to accept, for instance, that Jesus Christ spoke in parables; what we haven't yet accepted is that anyone speaking *about* Jesus Christ also speaks in parables. Anyone speaking to God or about God has to learn another language, a language of silence, symbolism, mystery or myth. Rather than de-mythologising scripture to conform to our ways of knowing, we should be re-mythologising ourselves to encounter what is happening therein.

MYTH AND MENOPAUSE

Myth as a third way of truth between fiction and fact is not just an addition to our epistemological armoury; it is an essential compass to guide us, especially as we negotiate the perils notoriously associated with the second half of life. Leaving our youth behind and entering gracefully the charms of adulthood is something of an exodus in itself. We need a mythological backup to prepare us for the journey.

We live in a world that denies the reality of death and tries both to hide it and to hide from it. When I wished an elderly friend of mine in America a happy birthday, she replied: "we don't have birthdays here anymore, my dear, we have face-lifts." We glory in a world of youth and beauty and try to persuade ourselves that this is the way life was intended to be. Advertisements which ambush us from every side insist that youth can be everlasting. More and more people are living the glory days of their prime as far into the future as they can. Sixty is the new forty; OAPs not travelling the world are missing out. I find myself becoming more and more exhausted from constantly urging to victory in grand slams a tennis player whom I hugely admire, but who will be approaching forty in the year this book is published.

Where do we stop? And when do we begin the second half of our life? Our aim seems to be to remain as young and beautiful as possible, even in death. The beauty industry around our bodies in a coffin is infamously unrealistic. 'She or he looks fantastic' we say to ourselves disbelievingly in funeral parlours. Our culture promotes and applauds every attempt to remain young and fit and impossibly healthy right into middle age. Last year, 2018, Man Kaur, a 101-year-old woman from India, won the gold medal in the 100 metre dash at the World Masters Games in New Zealand.

Admittedly, she was the only participant in the 100-and-up age group, but, according to the media "she is a rock star". Being a rock star and running 100 metres on your 100th birthday seems to be a legitimate aspiration. Supercentenarians are on the up. At least 100 people are registered as 110. One of these was asked if there were any advantages whatsoever to being 110 and she is supposed to have replied: "Very little peer pressure."

Now, of course, there's nothing wrong with living your youth to the full for as long as you can, but the more important thing is to cope with what's coming afterwards.

We would free up gigantic health resources if we were prepared to accept that death is a natural and even, at times, desirable process. Nearly 90% of the money spent in the health service in England, I am told, is apportioned to the last three months of life,[25] mostly trying to 'do more' for patients whose time is up. This comes, sometimes, as pressure from families who insist on their right to life, that there must be more that can be done: 'I hope you are not giving up on my parent.'

Those of us who really believe that there is a life to come, have a different view of death, which implies that we should not torture the elderly unnecessarily, and without much hope of curing them. Instead we should be preparing them as much as possible for a peaceful death, a hopeful transition to another kind of existence. So many people are prevented from dying with dignity by unwarranted attempts to keep them alive at all costs. The art of 'dying well' has been widely discussed in such areas as gerontology, palliative medicine, and care of the terminally ill. Most studies in these fields have concluded that a 'good death' is often linked with a spiritual outlook that sees death as part of the broader life of the spirit.[26]

....

25 This information comes from a conference in Northern Ireland in 2016 where Dr Klaus-Martin Schulte presented these facts.

26 David Tacey, *Gods and Diseases*, HarperCollins, Sydney, 2011, p. 80 (Much of what I say in the following paragraphs is what I have learned from this book. I have placed a number in square brackets at the end of sentences which refer to pages in Tacey's work which can expand the point we are both trying to make.)

Who can teach us how to die, not just physically but 'to our natural self' so that we can be reborn to our spiritual self? Such, as I see it, is the purpose of the mid-life crisis and also the 'usefulness' of spiritual vision. The second self serves the needs of the second half of life. And we have to give birth to this second self spiritually. We stand in the gap between what we are and what we could be. This used to be (and still is for some) the task of religion: to offer our consciousness goals to strive for, and myths to live by. We are being introduced to another way of being and knowing. We have to learn humility before a mystery which we cannot comprehend rationally. We must allow ourselves to be 'led' by the unconscious towards a new realm of experience.

The goal of the second half of life is to realise (that is 'to make real') your other half, your spiritual as well as your bodily personality. In terms of your sexuality, for instance, the purpose in the second half of life is not to propagate the species but to give birth to the soul, which for many of us is the most difficult birth of all. If we do not live in a mature culture with spiritual goals and pathways, we will not know how to grow old with grace and wisdom. Instead of becoming elders, dignified by, and valued for, our wisdom, we simply become old people, and a burden on a society that prefers youth and achievement. When spiritual goals are absent, old age becomes a tragic and a negative process. We experience the loss of vitality with a nostalgia that leads to depression; we live the second half of our life in relentless pining for the good old days. Surrender is difficult for the ego, unless it is aided by tribal wisdom, religious culture, or somehow becomes attuned to the demands of the spirit.

If we are assailed by suicidal impulses it can be as a desperate response to the real need which is to release a larger life. Consumerism and materialism in this perspective are symptoms of our unfulfilled life. We long to have *more*, but the 'more' we want cannot be supplied by an accumulation of 'worldly' goods. Shopping, we are told, has become the fourth greatest addiction.

In 1964, Russ Wlliams, a Texas oil businessman got the idea to open 'mini-warehouses' called the 'A-1 U-Store-It U-Lock-it U-Carry-the-Key'.

The first one was just 100 feet by 30 feet and was painted yellow and black to catch people's attention. The idea caught on so fast that he couldn't keep up with the demand. Now 53,000 storage facilities in the US have created a $22 billion a year business which works out as an increase of 740% in last 20 years. We amass 'things' we don't need and the storage space for such excess baggage has proliferated exponentially even in our own homes. Generally, after six months the cost of storage exceeds the value of the items.

Crossing the divide between youth and age has become for our culture a journey of mythic proportion. The word menopause (a combination of the Greek words for 'moon' and 'cessation') was coined to describe the time when a woman's menstrual periods stopped permanently and she could no longer get pregnant. More recently the term has been extended to incorporate the experience of 'mid-life crisis' which is common to all of humanity. The terms 'male menopause' or 'andropause' have become buzz words in the popular media in an attempt to become inclusive. Some men in their late 40s and early 50s develop depression, loss of libido, erectile dysfunction, and other physical and emotional symptoms which parallel the much more definitive and explicitly physical realities involved in a woman's menopause.

From a spiritual point of view, the childbearing age is over and the capacity to give birth to an actual child in the real world has to be transformed into the inner productivity which we call giving birth to 'our inner child,' to ourselves spiritually as 'children of God.'

> I have treated many hundreds of patients. Among those in the second half of life – that is to say, over 35 – there has not been one whose problem in the last resort was not that of finding a religious outlook on life. It is safe to say that every one of them fell ill because he had lost that which the living religions of every age have given their followers, and none of them has really been healed who did not regain his religious outlook.[27]

....

27 C.G. Jung, *Modern Man in Search of a Soul*, Harcourt, Brace & Co., New York, 1934, p. 264.

This is Carl Jung writing towards the end of his life during which he established his version of psychoanalysis as an attempt to offer some kind of equanimity to his contemporaries. The aim of all such psychotherapy, according to Jung, is to assist the individual in reestablishing a healthy relationship to the unconscious, neither getting flooded by it, which could describe any psychosis, such as schizophrenia, nor wrong-footed by it, which happens with neurosis, bringing depression, anxiety, and personality disorder. All of which happens to lives devoid of some deeper meaning.

We are facing as never before a spiritual crisis. There are now seven billion people on our planet, each one getting older every day. The religious and societal frameworks which used to help people advance through the various stages of their lives are on the wane; as we become more affluent and aware of ourselves, we become more impatient and more demanding. We are no longer governed by laws or taboos and we reach for whatever we find immediately satisfying with greedy impunity. Besides ageing and death, there is a terrifying spectre that haunts our society every day in the shape of incest, sexual harassment, and child abuse. On an hourly basis, our information technology is full to bursting with new revelations. It is no longer simply the Church and State institutions that are rife with such pathology, and sometimes criminality, the worlds of politics, sport and entertainment are proving vulnerable to such scrutiny. It seems as if child abuse has reached pandemic proportions. Probably the most prevalent and least reported epicentre for child abuse may turn out to be the family, which, for perfectly understandable reasons remains a secret.

Such, as I understand it, is the panic-stricken and pathological way that people, without any normative experience of the spiritual, try to activate the desire to be reborn to a new self.

We can substitute the interior, symbolic, and spiritual work of rebirth in ourselves for a crass literal activation of such desire, which we then inflict upon unsuspecting people in the real world. As an adult, we can attach the psyche's desire for rebirth, for reconnection (a translation for the Latin word *religio*) to an actual child, youth, or sibling, with whom we become obsessed, when in reality he or she is a symbol of our own need for rebirth as a child or a renewed self. The dearth of spiritual guidance and the demand for immediate physical gratification which characterise many of our present-day societies and cultures lead towards exploitation of the young, the defenceless and the vulnerable.

However, we must recognise that this crisis is universal. It exists within each one of us as much as it afflicts society as a whole. There is no point in throwing up our hands and issuing condemnations of the perpetrators as if they were a different species from ourselves. They are each one of us writ large. To use the condemned paedophile as a scape-goat and to lead the howling mob to the guillotine where punishment is to be exacted without mercy, is to refuse to deal with the real problem. This is an epidemic which affects us all, and unless we find both the symptom and the cure within ourselves we have skirted the issue and postponed the day of reckoning.

The key to such spiritual rebirth, as Jesus explained to Nicodemus in the third chapter of John's Gospel, lies in our ability to comprehend the mystical potency of the incest motif. Such desire for rebirth, such longing to become a new person has been identified as primary by most religions, and it can never be a return to the mother's womb, nor any surrogate substitute for such a return. The aim of both religion and psychology should be to encourage the sufferer of addictive, perverse or pathological behaviours to 'see through' the compulsion, recognise the 'spiritual' aim of such compulsion, and, rather than act out the instinctual impulse in a crude, literal, physical assault on an actual person of whatever age, to transform this desire into another kind of reality at a spiritual level, through ritual or symbolic action, which can release a rebirth of soul.

Fierce debates continue to rage in society, and in our law courts, about whether some of these incest attacks occur in reality, or whether they are invented at times by mentally compromised patients. The debate has polarised the community and the professions, giving rise to a cohort of outraged activists who argue that the incest epidemic is real, and being covered up by conservative social forces. On the other hand, a tradition of medical opinion has given rise to the view that a 'false memory syndrome' can be in operation, and we should not incriminate those accused of such crimes based on evidence supplied by those who are mentally unstable [126].

A case in point is the 1987 Cleveland child abuse scandal, which brought to public attention a wave of suspected child sexual abuse cases in the UK. From February to July of that year, many children living in Cleveland were removed from their homes by social service agencies and diagnosed as having been sexually abused. As there were not enough foster homes in which to place the allegedly abused children, social services began to house them in a ward at a local hospital. In May 1987, parents marched from the hospital where their children were being held to the local newspaper. The resulting media coverage caused the social service agency's practices to receive public scrutiny. In response, the Butler-Sloss report was commissioned by the Secretary of State for Social Services in July 1987 and published in 1988. It concluded that most of the diagnoses were incorrect. As a result, 94 of the 121 children were returned to their homes. On October 14th, 1991, the Children Act of 1989 was implemented in full as a result of the Cleveland scandal and other related incidents. In 1997 a TV documentary called *The Death of Childhood* alleged that "independent experts under the guidance of the Department of Health later found that at least 70% of the diagnoses" were correct. Such incidents reflect the panic which has invaded societies all over the world at the spectre of this pandemic of child abuse. We try to exaggerate or to dismiss it; we vilify the perpetrator and see evidence of criminality in the most innocent of situations; we spread an atmosphere of distrust around every child on the planet.

Such situations in the past were prevented (as far as we know) by socio-religious control. The incest taboo is almost synonymous with indigenous culture at certain points, and when this taboo breaks down it means we no longer have culture or religion to direct our energies towards spiritual goals.

The symbolic core of incest is rebirth. We are first born to our fleshly existence and our lives in the ego, but the unconscious expressed through various cultural myths impel us to search for a second birth, by which we become 'born again' of the spirit. The desire for such rebirth is natural, but nature does not supply us with the means by which it can happen. To find rebirth, we need imagination and culture. If we merely follow the path of instinct, it might suggest we achieve rebirth through sexual means, which leads on to criminal abuse of whoever we might force to become our correspondent.

It is our unconscious that makes the association of womb with rebirth. It is not an association that is conscious – in fact, the conscious mind of an incest perpetrator might find the idea of sexual relations with a family member abhorrent. But darker impulses of the unconscious and the disordered instincts can be activated, especially under the influence of alcohol or drugs. Under such conditions the incest taboo is weakened to such an extent that the suggestion that incest might be a path to personal rebirth leads the perpetrator to criminal action [122].

The way to incest is forbidden in every culture we have managed to record to date, and this prohibition exists universally precisely because we must be educated to search for a spiritual pathway to rebirth. Hence religions and myths are 'symbols of transformation,' in which we are prevented from carnal expression so that the spirit can be born. In many religious traditions, this reasoning is applied to sexuality more generally, not only within the family but also outside it, priestly celibacy being a case in point. We find such reasoning in Christian, Buddhist, Hindu and other traditions, and in every case the notion at the basis of celibacy is that the libido has to be damned up and sublimated into higher activity or striving [124].

Let us be clear: incest attacks are real and, if anything, under-reported. Incest is revealing of the nature of the psyche both as fantasy and as fact. Such reflection in no way excuses or condones the activity of rapists, sadists or child abusers, but it does point to the symbolic image, or impulse, which is at the core of such activity. And as psychologists and as spiritual directors, we must address this symbolic core of the problem, and if we don't, then no resolution can take place [132].

Psychologists, therapists and community workers can warn perpetrators of the crime; law enforcers can mete out prison sentences to terrify offenders; severe punishment or social reprimand can lessen the extent of such criminality; but none of these in themselves can suggest how the offending act could be transformed into a profound symbolic experience or a spiritual revelation. The perpetrator of the crime has to be made to see that he is seeking his own renewal or rebirth in such acts. Blinded by the image of the youthful self, the abusers do not perceive the child's distinct, separate reality and are completely insensitive to the child's individual needs. But no real cure can arise from simply admitting wrongdoing, enforcing punishment, and indulging in moralistic condemnation. We need to consider that spirituality alone can free us from the tyranny of this kind of criminality. Our punishing, moralistic, humanistic society cannot solve the incest epidemic but merely suppress or deny it, unless they undertake the spiritual work of directing such perpetrators towards a transformation of their real desire.

Modern society is paying a high price for abandoning the symbolic life, whether this was encased in a religious or a spiritual framework. Without any such cultural or religious outlet, the psyche will resort to pathologies to express its interior life and impulse.

In a purely secular culture, we do not know how to transcend the normal state of consciousness, except through eating, drinking and various kinds of substance abuse. We have to find a way of hoisting ourselves out of the merely natural, biological, material level of existence. Such a hoist was supplied in the past by cultural taboo or religious education. We need to find a corresponding substitute in some shape or form to allow ourselves the privilege of a fully human way of life. Instinctual impulse and sexual gratification must be allowed to aspire to another level which incorporates and does justice to our spiritual being. Whether we call this hoist 'religion' or transcendental psychology, or archetypal mythology, or symbolic transformation, the name is not important but the structure is essential. Our society must provide itself with access to a reality beyond our immediate workaday world.

UNSCRAMBLING THE MYTHO-POETIC

> Give the poem another day's drenching in the old brain,
> where thought and feeling intersect, till the voice of the
> poem has the pulse of the heart.[28]

Don't be put off by the terminology. I am trying to create a word that we
can agree upon to describe the way in which we can express the mythic
dimension. We could decide to use the initials MP for what we are trying
to describe, or we could create a composite word like 'mypo,' unless we
can come up with something more appropriate. As it is, the word is trying
to describe the ways in which we can translate the mythic aspect of our
experience into audible visible forms that can be recognised and utilised
in our everyday world. The word 'poetic' comes from the ancient Greek
word for 'doing' or 'making'. It encompasses more than poetry as such; it
could be music or dancing or film or ritual or any kind of language which
might provide what T.S. Eliot calls an "objective correlative" for whatever
mythic experience we are trying to describe.

When Jacob was wresting with the angel or when Moses approached
the burning bush or when Mary experienced the Annunciation, these
were inexpressible experiences never before encountered by humankind.
Words had to be found which could pass into our vocabulary to
domesticate these abnormalities. Now we talk of 'wrestling with the
angel' or encountering our 'burning bush' as illustrations to describe
outlandish circumstances in our daily lives. What was once beyond all
comprehensibility has taken its place in our cultural wardrobe. The myth
has become a metaphor.

....

28 Richard Murphy, *In Search of Poetry*, Clutag Press, Banbury, 2017, p. 59.

The particular avenue towards 'truth,' which I am calling the 'mytho-poetic,' derives from the kind of people we are on the one hand, and the kind of 'truth' we are presuming to approach on the other. In other words, it devolves from two extending parapets at either side of an abyss to be negotiated. On the one hand there is ourselves and the way in which our minds are constructed; on the other there is 'religion' and the possibility of reality beyond our ken.

The human brain is the product of over 500 million years of evolution. Apparently, the first structures and functions have not changed radically. The hindbrain being the oldest is the one we share with reptiles. This reptilian brain is nothing more than a bulbous protuberance from the spinal cord. This first part of the brain houses vital control centres that prompt breathing, swallowing and our heartbeat. It also holds the visual tracking system on which a frog relies to snap a dragonfly out of the air. It is our startle centre. Swift reaction to abrupt movement or noise perhaps caused this brain to sprout in the first place. This bulbous brain may have popped out of the spinal cord as a precaution against bushwhackery. At any event, the reptilian brain is steeped in the physiology of survival. The other two parts of our brain are less essential to the neurology of staying alive. As the brain evolved, new structures and functions were added until the model we presently enjoy displayed itself as tripartite. The second part, spread over the first, is sometimes called the 'limbic system,' or can be seen as the 'emotional' or 'Old Mammalian Brain'. It accrued as we left our reptilian status and developed our mammalian status about 150 million years ago.

The great divide between serpents and mammals is their reproductive system. Laying eggs or giving birth from inside your body changes everything about you. A new kind of relationship develops between the mother and child which, in turn, causes "a fresh neural structure to blossom within our skulls". This brand-new brain structure "transformed not just the mechanics of reproduction but the organismic *orientation* toward offspring". The reptile lays its eggs and slithers away indifferently.

The mammal nourishes and safeguards its young from the hostile world outside its group.[29] This second or *limbic* brain which drapes itself around the first is thereby more adapted to our emotional life. It has been called the 'visceral' brain and it connects the distant head with the throbbing heart. It is accompanied by a set of neural gadgets which link the two parts of the brain together.

The third storey is the newest and most spectacular development. It allows us to express ourselves in clear-cut abstract fashion. This neocortex (*neocortex* – Greek for 'new' and Latin for 'rind' or 'bark') is the last, and, in our case as humans, the largest of the three parts of the brain. We have the biggest neocortex-to-brain ratio of any other animal. It comes to us in such outsized proportion that it explains both our penchant for, and extensive capacity to, reason. For us, the latest and the newest tend to become the greatest and truest. We have become so enamoured of this most recent development that we ignore the other elements of our cranial make-up. The neocortical brain is not the most advanced of the three; it is simply the most recent. Because there is so much of it to include in a somewhat limited space, it shapes itself like two symmetrical sheets, each the size of a large, thick linen napkin, crumpled for better cramming into the small oblate shell of the skull. Like most of the brain, the neocortex is a warehouse of secrets and unanswered questions, but as it is the part of the brain which gives us our capacity to reason, we reduce it to that virtuosity and ignore its many other potentialities.

We need all three components of our brain and our maturity involves the correct balance afforded to each. The three are designed to interrelate. "Each brain has evolved to interdigitate with its cranial cohabitants." However, this is not the way things panned out. We live in a world which has discarded, to all intents and purposes, the first two parts of the brain and worships the third. Why not? It gives us our capacity to reason and

29 Thomas Lewis, M.D., Fari Amini, M.D., Richard Lannon, M.D., *A General Theory of Love*, Vintage Books, New York, 2000, p. 25.

gets us all the short-term rewards we covet. Not only do we ignore the first and second part of the brain but we focus our attention almost exclusively on only one half of the third part of the brain. We have, by now, become used to the distinction made by neuropsychologists between the left hemisphere of the brain and the right or 'minor' hemisphere which "was presumed, usually contemptuously, to be more 'primitive' than the left, the latter being seen as the unique flower of human evolution".

> And in a sense this is correct: the left hemisphere is more sophisticated and specialised, a very late outgrowth of the primate, and especially hominid, brain. On the other hand, it is the right hemisphere which controls the crucial powers of recognising reality which every living creature must have in order to survive. The left hemisphere, like a computer tacked onto the basic creatural brain, is designed for programmes and schematics; and classical neurology was more concerned with schematics than with reality, so that when, at last, some of the right-hemisphere syndromes emerged, they were considered bizarre.[30]

Writing in 1985, Oliver Sacks, from whom I have been quoting sporadically, suggested that "the entire history of neurology and neuropsychology can be seen as a history of the investigation of the left hemisphere".[31]

Auguste Compte (1798–1857) introduced the idea that human intelligence had developed from a primitive mythic stage, through a medieval metaphysical stage, right up to the scientific rationalism, which has so marked and transformed our world. This development was linear and rendered all stages that preceded it obsolete. But, there is no such evolutionary progress in a linear module, which casts off the previous in

30 Oliver Sacks, *The Man Who Mistook His Wife For a Hat*, Duckworth, London, 1985, p. 2.
31 Ibid. p. 2.

an advance towards the present, as a rocket might detach itself from the parts that launch it.

There is an older brain, where thought and feeling intersect and where our lives reverberate to the pulse of the heart. And we seem to have forgotten about it almost to the point of being ashamed of it. This book is an attempt to resuscitate that way of thinking, that way of being. It is an older way of inserting our lives into an ancient pattern, "pushing the music of dailyness against the shapes of the centuries," as Eavan Boland puts it. Those of us who are older know it off by heart: as it was in the beginning, is now and ever shall be, world without end. But there is a newer generation who might not have such a groove embedded in their psyche.

The other side of the bridge we are attempting to cross has been scored over the centuries by the various attempts made by humanity to scale these heights or plumb these depths. Religions of various kinds have tried to span this great divide and their efforts to do so have left remnants and elements that could be helpful to those coming after them. Christianity would claim to be a more proficient form of such architecture and yet, it too comes from the same side of the divide and carries many of the characteristics of the universal struggle of humanity.

Despite clamorous reports to the contrary, religion is alive and well in our world. Those who say that it is dying or dead, that 'secularisation' has taken over, are imposing their own 'dogmas' on an unsuspecting and gullible public. The 'facts' are clear: most of us are religious and can't help being religious. Being human means being 'religious', otherwise we die of depression or despair. Life is the first disease. Death is the second. Between them, they force us to hope. Religion is the way we cope with these three. Advocates of a more sombre, enlightened and realistic posture can tell us how immature we are, and how people living in the 21st Century should by now be cured of all these fantasies and superstitions, knuckling down to the hard facts of real life. If they think that their glum prognosis is gaining traction and that the world's population is gradually coming round to their point of view, they should take a look at their much vaunted statistics and take time to question the majority of real people who share the planet with them.

And 'religion' is not propositional, not a creed, to start out with. It is a deeply held conviction that begins with a story. The story is the virus that harbours and spreads the disease, which everyone is bound to catch because most of us are born into a family or bear a family of our own; and family is where we become inevitably infected with a particular brand of religion. The way such imagination is passed on is not by the channels of official Church teaching or by catechetical instruction, it is imbibed from the incubating breast of storytelling from which each of us as children and adolescents watched and listened to what was being conveyed to us through our living environment.

And of course we can deny or repudiate it later on. But the overwhelming evidence suggests that 'people' today are as 'religious' as ever, and are likely to remain so. Planning a new world, without taking this factor into account, is unrealistic.

There are many religions but one reality defines them all: a world beside, above, below or beyond this one.

> There are two worlds, 'the visible, and the invisible,' the world we see, and the world we do not see; and the world we do not see as really exists as the world we do see. The world we see we know to exist, *because* we see it. We have but to lift up our eyes and look around us, and we have proof of it: our eyes tell us. And yet in spite of this universal world which we see, there is another world, quite as far-spreading, quite as close to us, and more wonderful; another world all around us, though we see it not, and more wonderful than the world we see, for this reason if for no other, that we do not see it. [32]

32 John Henry Newman, *Parochial and Plain Sermons IV*, 208-11, Sermon 13; The Invisible World.

There is something 'more' than what we experience here in the short span between birth and death. That 'more' is a mystery. No one can claim to fully understand, let alone possess it. But most people are aware of it, and most of us need a religion of some sort to deal with it. There are, we are told, seven billion people in the world today and not more than 10% of these are registered as 'atheists' holding that no such other world exists. The other 90% have some belief in another world, another dimension, a reality that they might refer to as 'God'. One of Ireland's more feisty writers, Brendan Behan, declared himself "a daylight atheist," which might be a more honest account of where many of us stand. When the darkness and the mystery close in, we recognise that our definitive declarations at whatever level are bumptious. We know so little about anything that 'agnostic' might be a more accurate description of our knowledge about whether or not God exists.

People have been estranged from 'religion' in many ways and for different reasons; childhood experiences of churches and pastors that were damaging or abusive, teachings about God that were wrongheaded or plain daft. Many unnecessary stumbling-blocks have turned people away from sources of 'spirituality' that might have been, should have been, available to them. Some people now would rather die than come to terms with any notion of a divine presence. Our conditioning, certainly in Western-European society, has made us enemies of the spirit. Society at large, as most of us live in it today, especially in what we choose to call our 'developed' countries, is no friend to 'spirituality'. The notion of an afterlife, a life other and beyond the one we live, with a birthday each year counting down the time until we breathe our last, has fallen into disrepute mostly because of maudlin and improbable attempts to describe it.

REMYTHOLOGISING MYSTERY

After hundreds of years of being told that myth is false and the Gospels true because they are historically accurate, how can we retrace our steps? Could we now change tack without being seen as pusillanimous traitors by trying to introduce a new playing-field and a different set of criteria? Can we now rejig the narrative and bring people back to the place of the original question and persuade them to adopt a new approach? How can we now re-educate the multitude of staunch believers, who have so loyally defended all our incredible attempts to align our religious beliefs with current scientific norms? How can we back down and persuade them, and the lawyers of the Yellow-Eyed Hawk, that, of course, the Bible is written in the genre of myth, and was never intended to be otherwise; that it is not possible to replace myth with clear and distinct concepts; that, in order to understand the mysteries of any religion, especially of Christianity, we need to *participate* in the sacred, in ritual, in sacrament, and 'do' these things – through ritual enactment – in order to make present the reality which they invoke?

How can we show our contemporaries that myth is large enough, expansive enough, and sufficiently rooted in our psyches to enable a much-needed revitalisation of religious life? We have to leave the courtroom and bring the jury to another setting, in which we have to admit that entry is possible only through sacrament, poetry, music, iconography. The arts and imagination are probably the only way we can convey the sacred to today's disbelieving world.

As theologians we should take note: theology is a third hand exercise. The Church of Christ, for instance, is founded on a silent personal mystery, which can never be translated into human words. It is based on the Word made flesh. All speech about this reality is necessarily fumbling:

a stab at the truth. Tradition of the mystery (the way in which we hand it on) always risks betrayal. Christ came on Earth to reveal the mystery of that life which is lived eternally by the three persons of the Trinity. He replaced one mystery with another mystery. The only reality more mysterious than the three persons in one God is the reality of the human person. And this is the basis of the Christian religion, the mystery on which it is founded. When Pilate asked Jesus: "What is truth?" The answer was silence. The truth, in person, was standing in front of him. No more accurate or comprehensive embodiment of truth could have been present to him. The person is the only reliable expression of truth. Jesus Christ never wrote anything down Himself. The only recorded account of His writing was with His finger in the sand in front of the woman taken in adultery. So, any account of His life or His teaching is second hand. And all such accounts display glaring inconsistencies and irreconcilable disagreements.

The resurrection of Jesus Christ, which is the essential mystery upon which any faith in Christianity is based, was an unwitnessed event. No human person was present. Witnesses have testified to having seen His empty tomb; others claim to have met Jesus Christ in His resurrected humanity; but no one knows how or when His dead body was brought back to life.

Tradition for Christianity is the process whereby the mystery of Jesus Christ, the revelation of God's love in person, is transmitted by His followers. These followers are now organised into an official body called the Church. However, the truth that they transmit is ultimately derived from an oral preaching by the original bearers of this truth (which is no more and no less than privileged contact with Jesus Christ as the Risen Lord in person) passed on in many different ways through the ever-present agency of the Holy Spirit.

The word 'tradition' comes from the Latin for handing on, or handing over. In Greek the word is 'paradosis' which is used in the New Testament both for the way in which Judas 'handed over' Jesus as betrayal in the garden (Mark 14:10; 1 Cor, 11:23) and for the way Christians 'handed down' their beliefs (1 Cor, 15:3; 2 Thess, 2:15).

Every form and variety of tradition must travel the narrow path between these two translations. At every moment we can be betraying the truth and preventing people from seeing it. Tradition itself is free of every determination and cannot be contained in any formula, locality, or cultural manifestation; any historical embodiment limits it. Tradition in itself is silence and every word of revelation has a margin of silence. Certain nuggets hewn from this great silence have come down to us in both the Scriptures and liturgical tradition but as Ignatius of Antioch says (Ephesians 15:2) "The person who possesses in truth the word of Jesus can hear also its silence". If all the great silence of tradition had become scripture, St John tells us, "then the world itself would not be able to contain the books that would have to be written" (John 21:25). The silence is our turning towards the great abyss of divine love towards which every scrap of revelation, every detail of tradition, points.

Tradition as silence and as incomprehensible mystery translates itself into various traditions that help us to gain access to it. These can be found in certain human organisations, structures, documents, dogmas, formulae, creeds etc. They can materialise through councils of the Church, writings of theologians and doctors of the Church, canonical prescriptions, liturgical practices, devotional practices, iconography etc. But they are all secondary tributaries of the original silence of Tradition, which remains unwritten and mysterious. Tradition as such can never be found in itself in the horizontal tapestry of local and cultural traditions. In fact, Tradition is the way in which the Holy Spirit allows each one of the faithful to detect the mystery of Christianity within the length and the breadth of the 'horizontal' pattern of traditions. St Paul prays for the Ephesians (Eph 3:18) that they may be able to "comprehend with all the saints" not only what has become the "length and the breadth" of Revelation but also its "height and depth" which are never captured in the earthly forms.

Tradition from our point of view is more the unique way in which each of us is prompted to receive the 'words' of either scripture or liturgy, the symbols or the images of our cultural traditions, than it is any of those particulars in themselves. Ignatius of Antioch tells the Magnesians (8:2): "It is not the content of the Revelation but the light that reveals it; it is not the word but the living breath which makes the words heard at the same time as the silence from which it came." In this sense, tradition becomes more the Holy Spirit's gift of discernment to each of us, so that "those who have ears to hear with, may hear what the Spirit is saying to the churches". Tradition is no more or no less than the life of the Holy Spirit in the Church communicating to each one of us as persons, bestowing on us the faculty of hearing, of receiving, of knowing the Truth in the light which is divine. This is the knowledge of the truth that will make us free.

And yet we have to formulate the *mirabilia dei* into some enduring shape so that these are never forgotten and can be passed on from generation to generation.

However, like the written notation which preserves great musical works, the encoding is nothing without the music, which must be realised anew in every generation. Unless the music is actually heard it remains a disembodied skeleton in the score. Similarly, all creedal formulae, dogmatic tracts, articles of faith, articulations of the mysteries of Christianity, are humble servants of a much greater and quite other reality, which no person in the world can claim as a perfectly articulated possession. No person or people, church or catechism, dogma or denomination, completely incorporates the inexpressible mystery. Definitive incarnation took place only in the person of Jesus Christ. Post-Christian elaboration can only be the work of the Holy Spirit. The Spirit prompts and we babble. All that we 'know' about Christianity, about the Incarnation, about the Resurrection, about the Trinity, about the Eucharist, inhabits places in our hearts deeper than any words or definitions can reach. Our words are third hand attempts to sketch the unimaginable.

Karl Rahner suggests that our dialogue, as Christians, should concentrate on the future rather than on the past. If we try to develop together a theology of Christianity which will speak to the people of today and tomorrow this should help us to move closer together in the formulation of what we hold in common and what we understand as the mystery which unites us.[33]

Religare or religion means 'linking back,' establishing that connection to something other, something larger than ourselves, in whatever way is satisfactory for each person, so that it reaches the heart in a way that convinces. The proof is in the rightness of alignment, the way it sinks back perfectly into the socket. Otherwise we are flotsam on the changing tides of the continuum.

> If light, warmth, power, enjoyment and comfort are our primordial dreams, then modern research is science, permeated by the hard, courageous, mobile, knife-cold, knife-sharp mode of thought that is mathematics. We have gained in terms of reality and lost in terms of the dream. We no longer lie under a tree gazing up at the sky between our big toe and second toe; we are too busy getting on with our jobs . . . It is exactly as if that old-time, inefficient humankind had gone to sleep on an ant-hill, and when the new one woke up the ants had crept into its blood; and ever since then it has had to fling itself about with the greatest violence, without ever being able to shake off this beastly sensation of ant-like industry . . . Mathematics has entered like a daemon into all aspects of our life . . . but all those who know something of the soul bear witness to the fact that it has been ruined by mathematics and that in mathematics is the source of a wicked intellect that, while making us lord of the earth has also made us slaves of the machine.[34]

33 Karl Rahner, Theological Investigations, Vol. XIV, London, Darton, Longman & Todd, 1976, pp. 252-3.
34 Robert Musil, *The Man Without Qualities*, 1, Panther Books, 1968, p. 74.

PART III

PART III

MYTHICAL SPACE AND TIME

My awareness of mythology came from my childhood. I did not go to school until I was nine, as my American mother believed that children should not go to school until they themselves asked to do so. So the first decade of my life was spent roaming the hillsides of West Limerick. We lived on a farm and close by was Knockfierna, a large hill in the middle distance between us and the Galtee mountains, the third highest range in Ireland. If you were to situate it in ordinary space and time you might say that Knockfierna is in the County of Limerick, in the Republic of Ireland, eight degrees, 51 minutes and 23 seconds East of Greenwich and 52 degrees, 27 minutes and six seconds north of the Equator. Its National Grid reference is R469364. But this could not do justice to another reality. This reality is the one which was experienced by me as I climbed this hill. Wordsworth captures such reality more accurately in his poetry:[35]

> For nature then
> To me was all in all. – I cannot paint
> What then I was. The sounding cataract
> Haunted me like a passion; the tall rock,
> The mountain, and the deep and gloomy wood,
> Their colours and their forms, were then to me
> An appetite; a feeling and a love,
>
> But oft, in lonely rooms, and 'mid the din
> Of towns and cities, I have owed to them

....

35 William Wordsworth, 'Lines Composed a Few Miles above Tintern Abbey'.

In hours of weariness, sensations sweet,
Felt in the blood, and felt along the heart

While with an eye made quiet by the power
Of harmony, and the deep power of joy,
We see into the life of things.

It is through "sensations . . . felt in the blood" that an alternative kind of time and space allow us "to see into the life of things".

The countryside of Ireland, like that of Greece, is a network of mythological hiding places. Cnoc Fírinne (Hill of Truth) is a 900ft ridge of old red sandstone which rises abruptly from the limestone land of the surrounding area between the River Deel and the River Maigue. It has a cairn on top comprising a large heap of stones added to by those who climb the hill. This cairn is called an buachaill bréagach (the deceitful boy). Near it is an opening known as Poll na Bruíne which is an entrance to the underworld, the palace beneath the hill (Brú na Bruíne) where Donn Fíreannach presides.

The word Brú occurs sporadically in names of towns in the locality, Bruree and Bruff for instance. It refers to such underground hostels as are found at the great megalithic site in the Boyne valley known as Brú na Bóinne. These passageways to the underworld give space to the mythological mind. People around Ballingarry believe that there are underground tunnels from Cnoc Fírinne to the mouth of the Shannon, and up towards Tory Hill and beyond.

I later discovered that all cultures, and most children, around the world, believe in the existence of such a second dimension. I lived in Nigeria for three years and visited Australia in 2017, where the reality of mythological space and time are taken for granted.

He was speaking of poetry itself, of the hidden part it played in their lives, especially here in Australia, though it was common enough – that was the whole point of it – and of the embarrassment when it had, as now, to be brought into the light. How it spoke up, not always in the plainest terms, since it wasn't always possible, but in precise ones just the same, for what it deeply felt and might otherwise go unrecorded; all those unique and separate events, the little sacraments of daily existence, movements of the heart and intimations of the close but inexpressible grandeur and terror of things, that is our *other* history, the one that goes on, in a quiet way, under the noise and chatter of events and is the major part of what happens each day in the life of the planet, and has been from the beginning. To find words for *that*; to make glow with significance what is usually unseen, and unspoken too – that, when it occurs, is what binds us all, since it speaks out of the centre of each one of us; giving shape to what we too have experienced and did not till then have words for, though as soon as they are spoken we know them as our own.[36]

Aboriginal peoples have always lived this way which is the half-way house between the conscious and the unconscious. It is called Dreamtime by indigenous Australians. To understand myth is to learn another language, a very old language, but new to us. Archetypes or universal patterns are present in the myths and rituals of indigenous peoples. Jung claims these patterns have not been passed from culture to culture through external transmission but have arisen spontaneously from the collective unconscious. Myths deal with cosmic time and exemplary time rather than historical time.

....
36 David Malouf, *The Great World*, Chatto and Windus, London, 1990, pp. 283-4.

Harvard Art Museum held an exhibition in 2016 called *Everywhen*.[37] It took its name from an indigenous Australian concept better-known through its English translation as 'the Dreaming'. Everywhen was preferred because it emphasised time as a unity. For Indigenous Australians, past, present, and future overlap and influence one another in ways that defy Western notions of time. The Dreaming provides a way to understand and interact with past, present and future. "Our paintings are our memories for the future relatives." In narratives that are spoken, danced, sung, painted and safeguarded across generations, the Dreaming is made and remade as eternally present . . . in its singularity, sequentiality, and connectivity.[38]

Museums, among other cultural institutions, have not only historicised indigenous people, but at the same time have de-historicised them. Removed from history and erased from the present, indigenous people simply cease to be, leaving only their artefacts behind.

In their work, indigenous artists often draw on iconography from the ceremonies that punctuate indigenous life. While many ceremonies are performed less and less in their totality, artists often recall parts of them while painting: song cycles are sung, dances are gestured and the rhythm of ceremony is expressed through the movement of the brush. Artists will often paint for as long as the ceremonial performance would have lasted. Mark-making becomes the mechanism for honouring ceremonial time, and the act of painting brings the ancestral narratives into being, safeguarding them for the future. As Jennifer Biddle writes: "in so far as the Dreaming has an ontological status . . . it cannot be comprehended outside the acts which constitute it. These works which are *about* the Dreaming

37 *Everywhen: The Eternal Present in Indigenous Art from Australia*, edited by Stephen Gilchrist, Harvard Art Museums, distributed by Yale University Press, New Haven and London. This publication accompanied the exhibition on view at the Harvard Art Museums, in Cambridge Massachussets, from February 5 through September 18, 2016.
38 Ibid. p. 19.

literally bring the Dreaming *into being*. Ancestral potency arises within these paintings and is actively produced by them."[39]

For the viewer, the rhythm of ceremony is sensed through the forms and technique of the artwork. The fulcrum on which this system is balanced is the body itself. Body and country are active and activated by both the practice of ceremonies and the practice of painting. The exhibition was an invitation for us all to become synchronous with the Everywhen, if only momentarily. The Everywhen is everywhere. It is found in the dynamic of transformation, and is quickened through the mindfulness of ritual.[40]

Ritual is the idiom of myth. This is why from the earliest times of human history, people re-enacted their myths in stylised ceremonies. Religions were dramas or rituals of the soul.

In Africa the anthills of the Savannah were openings to an underground world. The Nigerian writer, Wole Soyinka, who won the Nobel Prize for Literature in 1986, bases many of his plays on ancient traditional rites and ceremonies taken from his Yoruba culture. Theatre becomes the x-ray machine that allows us to observe the bone structure of the world. Every item on the stage makes up, at one level, a recognisable geographical location, but, when loosened up and disentangled by music and dance especially, they become a deeper-laid contour map of another country. These plays open passageways to a world other than the one inhabited on a daily basis. Anthills in Nigeria, like fairy forts in Ireland, are openings into an alternative space inhabited by the dead, by the ancestors. Some of these plays are attempts to make present the spatio-temporal structure of this invisible world, contiguous to our own. The stage itself is carved into architecturally distinct areas at least one of which is the preserve of the in-between world. There is a symbolic quality to characters, events, stage properties, all of which act as the tip of a deeper reality. Soyinka's

....
39 Ibid. p. 24.
40 Ibid. pp. 27-30.

plays are passages which attempt to make visible the line or band that connects this world that we inhabit with the one inhabited by the dead and the unborn. "The confrontation in the play" he says of *Death and the King's Horsemen*, "is largely metaphysical, contained in the human vehicle which is Elesin and the universe of the Yoruba mind, the world of the living, the dead and the unborn, and the numinous passage which links all: transition."

In *Dance of the Forests*, the play performed as part of Nigerian Independence Celebrations in October 1960, and in *The Swamp Dwellers*, the forest and the swamp on stage represent that 'other' world, out of which can come those capable of making the 'transition' to our world. "The scene is a hut on stilts, built on one of the semi-firm islands" which mirror the kind of world we inhabit.

In his 1965 play *The Road*, "this symbolic feature is the numinous passage, the narrow ridge, the no-man's land between the land of the living and the abode of the dead". The mute Murano, who also limps, is a lost soul whose homeland is elsewhere:

> Deep. Silent but deep. Oh my friend, beware the pity of those that have no tongue for they have been proclaimed sole guardians of the Word. They have slept beyond the portals of secrets. They have pierced the guard of eternity and unearthed the Word, a golden nugget on the tongue. And so their tongue hangs heavy and they are forever silenced... When a man has one leg in each world, his legs are never the same. The big toe of Murano's foot – the left one of course – rests on the slumbering chrysalis of the Word. When that crust cracks, my friends – you and I, that is the moment we await. That is the moment of our rehabilitation.[41]

Murano, because he cannot speak in the idiom of our workaday

41 Wole Soyinka, *The Road*, in Collected Plays, Vol.I, Oxford University Press, 1973, pp. 186-7.

world, is the symbol, the embodiment of the artist who, in the Yoruba tradition, is one of those singled out to represent the other world:

> It is believed that the spirit of the deceased may be evoked to enter into the masquerade during the dance. At the height of the dance every true *egungen* will enter into a state of possession when he will speak with a new voice.[42]

The play is an enactment of the transition. One of the characters, the Professor, who is trying to understand these realities from our side of the transitions-line, gives an explanation of the role of Murano. Asked where he found Murano, he says that he found him "neglected in the back of a hearse and dying". He nursed him back to life and "set him to tap palm wine," which is a way of saying that he was tapping another source of truth. "The dance is the movement of transition . . . Agemo, the mere phase, includes the passage of transition from the human to the divine essence."

Maps in our day are becoming interactive and aware of constant flux. Perhaps they may begin to accommodate such alternative dimensions. Knockfierna itself was the palace of Donn Fíreannach, god of the dead and of the fertility of the land, who was generally seen in our area on horseback.

A cross-country hurling match between the Slua Sí of Cnoc Fírinne led by Donn and the Slua Sí of Lough Gur and Cnoc Áine (Knockainey) led by the goddess Áine took place every Autumn. The ball would be thrown in half-way between the two places, about 15 miles between Knockfierna and Knockainey. If Donn succeeded in driving the ball back to Knockfierna the crops in this part of the country would thrive, but if Áine got the upper hand the people of Ballingarry could look out for themselves.

---

42 Ulli Beier, *Year of Sacred festivals in one Yoruba Town*, Lagos, 1959.

There is an account of Cearúil Ó Dálaigh (composer of *Eilín a Rún*) travelling to Kilmallock to get Eilín to elope with him: he noticed a white horse going up the hill of Cnoc Fírinne. He followed it to the Poll Dubh where he found a horse grazing but no sign of its rider. He threw a stone down the Poll na Bruíne. It was thrown back hitting him in the face and breaking his nose.

An old man who worked for my father told me that coming back from church in Granagh he heard 'fairy' music. As he looked through the low open window of his room out on Knockfierna, he knew that he would be there soon on the whale-backed Black Hill beside. It is the opening offered through Poll na Bruíne that needs to be investigated.

When eventually I did go to school, I was surprised that the teachers had no interest whatsoever in Donn Fíreannach or his buachaill bréagach. In fact, they regarded all that as nonsense at the best of times and as heresy at the worst of times. And they had their ways of dealing with heretics. Every teacher in the school was armed with a different kind of weapon for beating out heresy and converting pagans. Pagans and Heathens, I later learned, were all those who lived in the countryside (*paganus*) and dwelt on the heaths. At school there was only one world. It was measured by geometry (which means, in Greek, 'measuring the world') and counted in numbers which contained no magic. We sat in serried rows as passive clones for nine hours every day, supervised for the most part by one other person who brainwashed us continuously. The object was to help us 'get ahead' in the workaday world. We learned to read and write and then began the scientific conquest of the space-time continuum in which we lived. There was one kind of space and one kind of time. Both were absolute and invariant. There was no question of space being beyond us or time being inside us, no understanding of my space or your space, no appreciation of music as time being 'felt' or made audible, no such thing as time-for-us. This was an inventory of intelligible locations and dates, a map of the world for anthropologists anonymous. If you were living in any other kind of space and time, you were a dreamer, an idler, a good-for-nothing. The space we all lived in was an ordered totality of concrete extensions, the time we lived in was an ordered totality of concrete durations. Space, time and motion had been calculated for us; all we had to do was learn off the formulae. There was no time or space for an overworld or an underworld, we were dealing with the 'real' world. We measured this in metres, kilograms, and seconds. It didn't matter what anyone felt like, or what was going on underneath the ground. All that was subjective and personal. What we were after was an objective assessment: a picture of the world from nobody's point of view.

By the time I left school, of course, this attempt to reduce the world to signs and symbols which were unambiguous, incontravertible and universally accepted, had already been changed. Just after my 16th birthday the standardised MKS of my rigid schooldays had been revised. The mouth of the Poll Dubh on Cnoc Fírinne was now to be measured in metres which were more accurately and scientifically accepted to be 1,650,753.73 wavelengths of the orange-red light of krypton 86.

MYTHOLOGISING HISTORY

Sometimes we turn history into myth. Things that happen locally and incidentally become magnified and enlarged to form templates of heroic achievement. The great escape, the fight against the dragon, the move from rags to riches, these archetypal stories begin as unremarkable biography. And as we all inhabit time and space, our movement from the womb to the outside world, from the dining room to the drawing room, from home to school, become the basis for our most extravagant accounts of journeys we have made, whether as *Wanderly Wagon* through the prairie or in *Star Trek* though the galaxy. If our journey is one in which we set out and never come back it takes on the mantle of an Exodus; if it travels for miles and eventually gets us home it qualifies as an Odyssey. In any event it raises the historical to the level of a myth.

Judeo-Christianity itself emerged from the exodus. This became the identifying myth, the defining symbol of the march towards freedom, which, in terms of our human condition, has to mean progress towards what is unlimited and unconditional. Before this unimaginable event there was no people of Israel. The exodus from Egypt constituted the people of Israel. Before that event there was nothing but a scattering of disconnected people with no history, no reality, no identity. The exodus became the founding myth, the liturgical contour of the historical people. Even the account of the creation of the world in the book of Genesis, experts tell us, is a retrospective projection of the contours of the exodus experience onto the imagined emergence of the cosmos from chaos. The pivotal point in Israel's liturgical life is the continued reassertion of the astonishing claim that "...Yahweh rules, and therefore the world can act out its true character as God's creation".[43]

....
43 Walter Brueggemann: *Israel's Praise*, Philadelphia, Fortress Press, 1988, pp. 26-28.

Martin Buber describes the possible emergence of the original Paschal liturgy, the way in which the exodus was celebrated liturgically, as follows:

> Favourable circumstances have, within a relatively brief period, provided a man possessing the character and destiny of a leader with the external prerequisites for the fulfilment of his immediate task, the leading of a group of semi-nomadic tribes out of the land of 'bondage'. The geographical and political conditions under which the impending wandering has to take place are tremendously difficult, no matter whether that wandering already aims at landed possession and settlement or, for the time being, at the resumption of a nomadic life. The human groups whom he proposes to lead out are only loosely associated with each other; their traditions have grown faint, their customs degenerate, their religious association insecure. The great thought of the man, his great impulse, is to establish a covenant of the tribes in the purer and freer atmosphere of the desert, which had once purified and freed him himself. And so Moses reintroduces the holy and ancient shepherds' meal, renewed in meaning and form.[44]

The essential thing to realise, Buber suggests, is that here a natural and customary human activity, that of eating, is elevated by the participation of the whole community to the level of an act of communion; and as such is consecrated to God, is eaten 'for him'. However, such religious symbols cannot be merely arbitrary, or the specified protocol of some charismatic religious leader. They grow out of the individual or collective unconscious and, as Paul Tillich has suggested, "cannot function without being accepted by the unconscious dimension of our being". This is what makes liturgical symbolism antecedent to, and more potent than, any rational organisation or explanation.

....
44 Martin Buber: *Moses: The Revelation and the Covenant*, Harper Torchbooks, New York, 1958, pp. 69-72.

'Out of what womb are symbols born?' Out of the womb which is usually called today the 'group unconscious' or 'collective unconscious,' or whatever you want to call it – out of a group which acknowledges, in this thing, this word, this flag, or whatever it may be, its own being. It is not invented intentionally; and even if somebody would try to invent a symbol, as sometimes happens, then it becomes a symbol only if the unconscious of a group says 'yes' to it. It means that something is opened up by it.

Tillich holds that religious symbols do exactly the same thing as all symbols do, which is "open up a level of reality which otherwise is not opened at all, which is hidden". But this is not enough. If they are to reach the depths of reality that can be termed 'religious' they have to touch upon ultimacy. "We can call this the depth dimension of reality itself, the dimension of reality which is the ground of every other dimension and every other depth, and which therefore, is not one level beside the others but is the fundamental level, the level below all other levels, the level of being-itself, or the ultimate power of being."[45]

Martin Buber admits that we do not know what the original meaning of the term *pessah*, translated as 'Passover,' may have been.

> The interpretation of the 'leaping over' the houses of Israel by Yahveh, the 'destroyer' during the night of the death of the first-born is, in any case, secondary; even though at the time of Isaiah this supplementary meaning had become established. The verb originally meant to move on one foot, to hop. It may be assumed that at the old nomad feast a hopping dance had been presented, possibly by boys masked as he-goats. Just as there are war dances in which the desired event is portrayed and simultaneously trained for until the mime suddenly becomes a

45 Paul Tillich, *Theology of Culture*, New York, Oxford University Press, 1959, pp. 58-59.

reality, so, it may be imagined, a symbolic representation of the Exodus may have passed into the Exodus itself.

This suggests that the 'symbol' was both the initiation and the repercussion of what eventually transformed itself into the exodus event. In other words, the intuition that Yahweh was trying to inspire in his people was delivered through a ceremonial rite, a dance, almost as a dream can provoke the daylight action to which it acts as prelude.

> Moses transformed the clan feast of the shepherds (the unleavened flat cakes are the bread of the nomads) into the feast of a nation, without it losing its character of a family feast. And now the families as such are the bearers of the sacramental celebration; which, however, unites them into a national community. Moses did not change the custom of the ages into a cult; he did not add any specific sacrificial rite to it, and did not make it dependent on any sanctuary; but he consecrated it to Yaveh. He transformed the already existent Passover by introducing a new sense and symbol, as Jesus did later by the introduction of a new sense and symbol.

"The liturgy, both in its totality and in each of its rites or actions, is symbol," Alexander Schmemann explains. But he makes an important distinction. Liturgy is "the symbol, however, not of this or that particular event or person, but precisely of the whole mystery". The mistake we have made is in applying to the liturgy a kind of symbolism which can be described as 'illustrative' which means treating the liturgy as a substance or a texture in which every element and every aspect has to be symbolic of some action or attachment attributable to the earthly life of Jesus Christ. On the contrary, "the entire liturgy is the symbol of the mystery of Christ's ascension and glorification, as well as the mystery of the Kingdom of God, the 'world to come".'[46] Where did this liturgical ritual spring from? Goethe's Faust aptly replies: "*Im Anfang war die Tat* (In the beginning was the deed)." 'Deeds' were never invented, they were done; thoughts, on the other hand, are a relatively late discovery. Ritual and liturgical expression come long before theoretical explanation or dogmatic theology.

What all of this is trying to accomplish is the insertion of divine life into the circumference of human life. Biological life is horizontal and circular: Time as birth, growth, decay, death. Resurrected life goes in the other direction. It introduces us to a different kind of space, *khora* instead of *topos*, as the Greek words describe, and to a different quality of time, *kairos* as distinct from *chronos*. Events rather than cycles are emphasised; milestones rather than metronomes; a freeze-frame tempo rather than a mere passage of time. We have to set our watches and our hearts to rise to such moments. Ready for ecstasy, poised for take-off. Putting in such a pacemaker is the work of liturgy. Exodus is the essential journey towards freedom. So many of our lesser attempts to free ourselves from whatever kind of oppression have been superimposed on this myth.

A concrete example: Paul Revere's ride to warn the Massachusetts' Provincial Council sitting in Concorde of possible British troop movement to capture their cache of military supplies. The metric space of geometry and mathematics require no more than the time he would have taken to travel on horseback the 16.34 miles from B to C. Which route did he take? How far did he go? How long did it take him? The rest, as far as scientific calculation is concerned, is pure sentimentality. Geometry and mathematics invent a space which is homogenous "which is never given space, but space produced by construction". But my space and your space doesn't come in 'one size fits all'; nowhere in the space of lived reality can such homogeneity be achieved. The metrics of Henry

....
46 *Liturgy and Tradition, Theological Reflections of Alexander Schmemann*, edited by Thomas Fisch, New York, St Vladimir's Seminary Press, 1990, pp. 39-40.

Wadsworth Longfellow in 'Paul Revere's Ride' lead us on an alternative mytho-poetical journey.

> Listen, my children, and you shall hear
> Of the midnight ride of Paul Revere,
> On the eighteenth of April, in Seventy-Five:
> Hardly a man is now alive
> Who remembers that famous day and year.
>
> A voice in the darkness, a knock at the door,
> And a word that shall echo forevermore!
> For, borne on the night-wind of the Past,
> Through all our history, to the last,
> In the hour of darkness and peril and need,
> The people will waken and listen to hear
> The hurrying hoofbeats of that steed,
> And the midnight message of Paul Revere.

If we do choose to take a scientific point of view we may be disenchanted by Longfellow's abuse of historical fact: Paul Revere was not waiting 'booted and spurred' in Charlestown across the river from Boston for the signal - those famous lanterns hung in Christ Church tower to indicate that British troops had left Boston - he was still in Boston when the signals were shown. Neither did he ever arrive at Concord. He was captured outside Lexington.

'Mythical space' is more closely related to the space of sensory perception than to the logical space of geometry. Like the ordinary spaces in which we live our daily lives, every part of our living rooms have their own distinct 'mode' and 'value'. "In contrast to the homogeneity which prevails in the conceptual space of geometry every position and direction in mythical space is endowed as it were with a particular accent."[47]

47 Ernst Cassirer, *The Philosophy of Symbolic Forms*, Yale University Press, 1955, Volume 2, pp. 83- 85.

Longfellow, like Homer was creating a foundation myth, using an account of an otherwise obscure messenger's ride in 1775 almost 100 years later in 1860, "to warn the American Union that it was in danger of disintegrating (which it was)"[48] at the time when he was writing the poem.

> Epic is not an act of memory, not merely the account of what people are able to recall... nor is it a kind of history, an objective laying out of what occurred in a past to which we have little or no access. Epic, which was invented after memory and before history, occupies a third space in the human desire to connect the present to the past... to make the distant past as immediate to us as our own lives. To make the great stories of long ago beautiful and painful now. Nothing is more insubstantial than poetry. It has no body, and yet it persists with its subtleties whole, and its sense of the reality of the human heart uneroded. Nothing more lasting. Homer, in a miracle of transmission from one end of human civilisation to the other, continues to be as alive as anything that has ever lived.[49]

Historical incidents, from the mytho-poetic point of view, were not seen as unique occurrences but were thought to be external manifestations of constant timeless realities. Hence history would repeat itself. Such narratives tried to bring out this eternal dimension (by finding the appropriate myth or symbol for the occasion) and placing history in the realm of spirit. Ancient literature strove to depict in myths and dramas the eternal norms of life experience.

Every one of us has, or is, a Paul Revere in our lives. The ride for freedom is universal and archetypal. A few miles from where I lived in Co. Limerick, Ireland, we celebrate 'Sarsfield's ride,' at Ballyneety near

48 https://www.biography.com/news/paul-reveres-ride-facts
49 Adam Nicholson, *The Mighty Dead, Why Homer Matters*, William Collins, London, 2014, p. xix-xx.

Pallasgreen. In the early hours of Tuesday August 12th, 1690, General Patrick Sarsfield with the pick of the Irish cavalry, rode a similar mythic trail and, invading the English camp, destroyed a siege train bound for Limerick. The password of the English troops was 'Sarsfield' which prompts our poem to end:

> A tramp of horse: "Whose there? The Word?"
> "Sarsfield!", the answer ran,
> And then the sword smote downwards,
> "Aye, and Sarsfield is the man!"[50]

Every culture has a Paul Revere or a Patrick Sarsfield and celebrates their mythic rides towards freedom.

Perhaps the most famous of such poems is Robert Browning's 'How they Brought the Good News from Ghent to Aix,' which tells a similar story in 1845, fifteen years before Longfellow.

> I sprang to the stirrup, and Joris, and he;
> I galloped, Dirck galloped, we galloped all three;
> 'Good speed!' cried the watch, as the gate-bolts undrew;
> 'Speed!' echoed the wall to us galloping through;
> Behind shut the postern, the lights sank to rest,
> And into the midnight we galloped abreast.

The poem is more about galloping than it is about Ghent, and Browning himself remarked in a letter, "There is no historical incident whatever commemorated in the poem... a merely general impression of the characteristic warfare and besieging which abound in the annals of Flanders." (Letter dated 1883).

....

50 'Galloping Hogan' from *Prose, Poems and Parodies of Percy French*, ed. Alfred Perceval Graves, Dublin, The Talbot Press, 1962, pp. 33-35.

During the 20th Century the Yellow-Eyed Hawk often persuaded the tendency to go in the opposite direction. The attempt was made to turn myth back into history. The 19th Century finds of Heinrich Schliemann (6th January, 1822 – 26th December, 1890) in Greece were given sensational status because of supposedly unearthing the geography of Homer. Most notable are the golden funerary masks of deceased Mycenaean nobles, especially the renowned Mask of Agamemnon, which has come to be called the Mona Lisa of pre-history.

The telegram sent by Schliemann to King George I of Greece, written in Greek on the 16th/28th November, 1876 is also on display in the National Archaeological Museum in Athens:

> Your Majesty, it is with great pleasure that I inform you that I have discovered the tombs which, according to Pausanias' account, belong to Agamemnon, Cassandra and their comrades who were murdered by Clytemnestra and her paramour, Aegisthus, during a feast. The tombs are enclosed within a double stone circle, something which would only have been erected in honour of exalted personages. Inside the tombs, I have discovered fabulous treasures and ancient objects of solid gold. These treasures alone are enough to fill a large museum which will become the most famous in the world and will attract myriads of foreigners to Greece from every land.

More recent archaeological research suggests that the mask is from 1550–1500BCE - earlier than the life of Agamemnon, as tradition regards it. But more sceptical books such as *Behind Agamemnon's Mask* suggest that it is a hoax! Proponents of this fraud argument centre their case on Schliemann's reputation for salting digs with artefacts from elsewhere. The resourceful Schliemann, they assert, could have had the mask manufactured on the general model of the other Mycenaean masks and found an opportunity to place it in the excavation. The extent of the historical basis of the Homeric epics has been a topic of scholarly debate for centuries. While researchers of the 18th Century had largely rejected the story of the Trojan War as fable, the theories and research of Schliemann made it plausible that the Trojan War cycle was at least remotely based on a historical conflict of the 12th Century BC, even if the poems of Homer were removed from the event by more than four centuries of oral transmission. Once again, the mytho-poetic is denied any reality unless it can be directly associated with historical fact.

MYTH AND MOVIES

What a dream is to an individual, myth is to a whole culture. It is as if the community dreams its genesis. And each culture, whether Babylonian, Scandinavian, Egyptian or Celtic, produce their mythologies from a recognisably similar cloth. Moreover, our dreams, whether dreamt by the ancients or our contemporaries, inhabit that same language. In the myth, as in the dream, impossible things happen which would be inconceivable in the real world of space and time. There are, of course, different dreams for each person and different myths for every culture, but what they have in common is that they all emerge as symbolic language. They refer to something other than themselves and they appear in the immediately accessible guise of a filmic story.

The difference between then and now is this: in the past both the personal dream and the cultural myth were of paramount importance. Failure to read either was the most serious and dangerous form of illiteracy. For the Yellow-Eyed Hawk of the mind both are regarded as irrelevant. They are no more than childish nonsense to be consigned to the dump while we as adults get on with the important business of living. It does not occur to our contemporary sensibility that both these manifestations are symbolic pointers towards a more balanced way of leading our lives and that they should be carefully scrutinised and interpreted. In our world today, artists are those who understand this language naturally and who are most likely to help us in our efforts to achieve some kind of fluency.

"When we are asleep we wake to another form of existence. We dream. We invent stories which never happened and sometimes for which there is not even any precedent in reality. Sometimes we are the hero, sometimes the villain... but whatever the role we play in the dream we are the author, it is our dream, we have invented the plot."[51] People who are dead appear and are real as they rub shoulders with others so much younger whom they never met. Others whom we would hardly remember in our waking consciousness appear and are so clearly delineated that we recognise them in every detail. Events that happened in childhood are juxtaposed with things that happened yesterday. And yet for all this apparent confusion with its anachronistic mismatch, we live the dream as it unfolds with intensity and conviction, as if it were for real. Also, it displays itself to us as if it were a film. It lays itself out visually before us. This is why cinema is so potent a carrier of symbolic language. Films, even if they have to bear subtitles, can be 'read' by audiences all over the world.

Cinema provided the perfect objective correlative to mythic thinking. Here was the world around us in immediate display. The great film theorist André Bazin claimed that cinema's photographic basis made it very different from the more traditional arts. By recording the world in all its immediacy, giving us slices of actual space and time, film puts us in a position to discover our link to primordial experience. Other arts rely on conventions whereas cinema goes beyond convention to reacquaint us with the concrete reality that surrounds us but that we seldom notice. As we watch a movie, we see a world unfolding which is comparable to the way in which we encounter the world from our earliest childhood. Having it served up in so tidy and compact a facsimile allows for fresh and detailed examination of day-to-day experience. Film is fundamentally the very matrix of mythic intelligence and it can catch us off guard before the whole cognitive processing of reality, which has become habitual to us through our 'literary' education, kicks in. But we still have to stop ourselves from pre-empting the immediacy of what we see by immediately translating it into the brail to which we have become accustomed. Almost as if we have to stop ourselves from inserting subtitles onto the screen instead of watching the unadulterated images.

....

51 Eric Fromm, *The Forgotten Language, An Introduction to the Understanding of Dreams, Fairy Tales and Myths*, Grove Press, New York, 1957, p. 4.

The novelty of realistically moving photographs was enough for a motion picture industry to mushroom before the end of the 19th Century. The year 1900 conveniently marks the emergence of the first motion pictures that can be considered as 'films', where basic editing techniques and film narrative were introduced. The first decade of the 20th Century found cinema moving from a novelty to an established large-scale entertainment industry. By the 1920s, the United States reached what is still its era of greatest-ever output, an average of 800 feature films annually, or 82% of the global total.[52]

Cinema is an art form, a medium, which did not exist before the 20th Century. It was, possibly, the only art form to have arrived before its own proper genius. Most other art forms were forced into being through irrepressible desire to express something in a fashion somehow adequate to the torrent of emotion pent up inside. Cinema came about through curiosity and technological inventiveness. It was a scientific feat which mesmerised the viewing public by its technical virtuosity. It was the inevitable result of a number of experiments which made it a container waiting for content; a medium before the message.

From the beginning it promised to be the perfect vehicle for the mythological mind. Pre-verbal, sensual, kinetic, it answered to the requirements of immediate physical connection with the world around us before the sophisticated gymnastics of cognitive abstraction set in. Here was life in the raw before it was chewed into logic by mind games we had learned so well. However, that was to underestimate the powerful influence of the Yellow-Eyed Hawk. From the beginning cinema was a most expensive way of expressing itself. The poet can write in a lonely room with a piece of paper and a pencil. Cinema involves several industries and hordes of skilled and highly paid people. From the outset it was dependent on huge financial backing and it veered between

....
52 Scott Eyman: *The Speed of Sound: Hollywood and the Talkie Revolution 1926-1930*, Simon & Schuster, New York, 1997.

popularity and propaganda to fill its coffers. It could become the tool of an ideological government or dance to the whim of a cinema going public. The director was so dependent upon patrons that many became puppets of the purse strings. From as early as the 1920s, films began to be divided into an entertainment cinema directed towards a mass audience and a serious art cinema aimed at a more intellectual audience.

Before the medium could assert itself and develop its own muscle and immediacy, it was pounced upon and adapted to suit the prevailing requirements of big business mass entertainment. The most potent paraphernalia for human self-expression was forced into the conduit for the 20th Century 'bread and circuses'.

Before its own original and specific artistry had time to articulate itself, transposed versions of other art forms were used to feed its waiting form. What began with a photograph, and developed into a series of shots melting into one another and simulating movement, was naturally conducive to the rhythms of literary narrative. The medium was ready for action and was fed with available fodder. Instead of recognising the ocular abundance which now presented itself, with corresponding expansion of the subtlety of the eye, moguls of the rapidly developing industry quickly closed down that dimension of the explosive medium they had to hand and sold it lock, stock and barrel to the less demanding needs of an already existing and voracious crowd pleaser. Rather than delaying over the sumptuousness of each image, the emphasis was placed on speed: image after image racing past to convey a story with beginning, middle and end. Each image became a vehicle for something other than itself, a mere carriage on the linear train of thought. Its only role was to disintegrate as fast as the eye could see, sacrificing its particular existence to the meaningful totality. Cinema became the equivalent of a 'page-turner' in the world of novels. And so novels and plays became the first films. It was as if the theatre was being relayed to a wider audience.

Cinema was to offer a cheaper, simpler way of providing entertainment to the masses. Filmmakers could record actors' performances, which then could be shown to huge audiences around the world. Travelogues would bring the sights of far-flung places directly to spectators' hometowns. Movies would become the most popular visual art form of the late Victorian age. And the name 'movies' describes the downward spiral. Films developed from a single shot of a single person taken by one other person with a few assistants, to full-length dramas made by large companies working with massive crews of actors and technicians in industrial conditions. By 1907 purpose-built cinemas for motion pictures were being opened across the United States, Britain and France. American films became increasingly attractive to audiences everywhere because of their sumptuousness and superior technical quality. By the 1920s, Charlie Chaplin, Buster Keaton and Douglas Fairbanks became household faces on every continent. All of this meant that the Western visual norm of the Yellow-Eyed Hawk became the pattern and the yardstick. From the beginning, the whole industry was galvanised to record the banalities of our already overplayed dramas, instead of allowing the medium to introduce us to the wonders of a new world.

This dilemma forced cinema to develop in two very different ways. The lines were drawn between popular commercial cinema and what became known as arthouse films. Directors, who saw the full potential of the new art form, shunned the temptations of popular success and developed their own kind of movie, which was praised by a small elite and ignored by the public at large. An art film is typically a serious artistic work not designed for mass appeal, aimed at a niche rather than a popular market, and made for aesthetic reasons rather than for commercial profit. Emphasis is placed on the director's authorial expressiveness; and there is usually focus on the thoughts, dreams or motivations of characters, as opposed to the unfolding of a clear, goal-driven story. The name of the director in such art movies is often more important than the names of actors and actresses which cover the billboards of commercial cinema and attract the average punter to the queue.

The boon to me in this regard was being sent to Paris to study philosophy and theology from 1966 to 1969. There, among all the other

benefits which accrued, was access to every form of art including the great
films which were being censored in other countries, especially in Ireland.
"Cinema's arrival in Ireland at the end of the 19th Century was broadly
contemporaneous with the establishment of a number of organisations
whose most explicit goal was the encouragement and development of
a distinctively Irish identity... While great efforts were made to achieve
this, still greater energy was expended in trying to restrict imported, most
especially English commercial entertainments and popular publications
which were deemed anathema to the Irish cultural nationalist project." [53]

From 1923, with the Censorship of Films Act, about 2,500 theatrical
films were banned in Ireland and between 10,000 and 11,000 were cut.
American movies became enemy number one. As James Montgomery,
the appointed censor of films from 1923 to 1940, often said: "one of
the greatest dangers of... films is not the Anglicisation of Ireland, but
its Los Angelesisation." The 1923 Censorship of Films Act was aimed
directly at the 'Harlotry of Hollywood'. Films banned in Ireland
included The Marx Brothers in *Monkey Business*, Charlie Chaplin's *The
Great Dictator* (Ireland being neutral at the time did not want to offend
Adolf Hitler), *Brief Encounter*, David Lean and Noel Coward's declared
masterpiece, and Joseph Strick's attempt to put Joyce's *Ulysses* on the
screen. If I had remained in Ireland, I would have been deprived of
the most immediate mythological initiation which arthouse cinema can
provide, as it was, I was introduced to the best European cinema from
Germany, Italy, Spain, and France as well as meeting personally, Luis
Buñuel and Robert Bresson.

Born on February 22nd, 1900, Buñuel became a master of cinema
as myth. One of his first films was *L'Age d'Or*, about the insanities
of modern life, the hypocrisy of contemporary bourgeois society,
and the value system of the Roman Catholic Church. The film is a

53 Kevin Rockett, *Irish Film Censorship, A Cultural Journey from Silent Cinema to Internet
Pornography*, Dublin, Four Courts Press, 2004, p.19.

series of vignettes, wherein a couple's attempts at consummating their romantic relationship are continually thwarted by the bourgeois values and sexual mores of family, Church and society. Right-wing French 'Patriots' interrupted the film by throwing ink at the cinema screen and assaulting viewers who tried to stop them. Spanish newspapers condemned the film as "the most repulsive corruption of our age". The film was withdrawn from commercial distribution and public exhibition for more than 40 years. 49 years later, from November 1st-15th, 1979, the film had its legal US premiere in San Francisco. It was one of the first items on a course I was following in Paris in 1967. It introduced me to the possibility of myth in the movies.

Buñuel was an entomologist before he became a director of films. *L'Age d'Or* opens with a documentary sequence showing the five sections of a scorpion's tail. These correspond to the five parts of the movie itself, where the last part contains the poison. The shape and symbolic structure of the scorpion's tail are pedantically displayed so that we can recognise them in the architecture of our daily lives, in the society we have constructed around ourselves. Two scorpions are put into a small box which resembles the hut which is the setting for the first scene of the film. What two scorpions do to each other in a match-box is what we do to each other in the prison-cells of our apartments, our railed side-walks, our cities.

Scene two is the foundation of the city, whether that be Rome or New York matters little. Every foundation is a repetition or Renaissance of The Age of Gold. Pilgrim fathers pay homage to skeletons on the rocks and then proceed to lay the foundation stone. Recognisable functionaries and dignitaries of our society stand solemnly around a square stone block on to which a small lump of fresh cement is delicately trowelled. Accompanying imagery leaves the viewer in no uncertainty about the identity of this 'cement'. We have built our city using excrement as cement. We imply that the amount of 'shit' in each human being (the foundation-stone of every society) is containable in the discreet lavatory bowls in bathrooms around the house. This serviceable portion can be used as cement to knit together the stones which create the ensemble. The 'cement' binds the structure into a permanent, coherent, all-embracing whole.

As the ceremony begins it is scandalously interrupted by a man and a woman rolling around in the mud as they try to achieve passionate copulation. This is the part of humanity which has to be locked up or stamped out, isolated or excluded, if the society under construction is to enjoy permanence and peace. The outcast has a dream: he sees the building under way making no provision for the torrent of excrement he harbours inside. These architects will no doubt provide somewhere in their building a sedate and discreet lavatory bowl deemed sufficient to contain the daily offerings of the local inhabitants, whereas the outsider sees a tidal wave of excrement descending on the bathroom which makes the roll of toilet paper on the wall curl up and disappear in dismay at the herculean task it is being asked to perform. The dissidents are removed and the ceremony continues. Rome is built in line with a psychoanalytical equation of gold and faeces; society as a golden cage is constructed and we are expected to adapt ourselves to its rigours and restraints. Where does all the scorpionic excrement go? The film shows it seeping into the walls and turning everything into inverted symbols of the scorpion's tail: railings, steeples, prison bars, wrought-iron gates, sky-scrapers, stretch in phallic lines to the horizon. The final scene (the poisoned tip) is a crucifix in a snow-storm with several scalps attached swaying in the wind. Christianity, for Buñuel is complicit in this construction of the Golden Age.

Robert Bresson (1907- 1999), in a small book called *Notes on Cinematography*[54]*12* written in 1975, makes a basic distinction between his work which he calls 'cinematography' and 'cinema' as most experience this art form to date. Cinema, according to him, is no more

....

54 Robert Bresson, *Notes on Cinematography*, New York, Urizen Books 1977 [referred to as NC in the text].

than photographed theatre, where everything is necessarily artificial. You don't expect to find real trees growing on the stage. Scenery is an artificial construction. Acting, in the idiom of theatre, has to participate in such artificiality. It is a calculated method. Cinema uses the camera to reproduce; cinematography uses it to create. Bresson hopes that cinematography can introduce us to something original, not merely photographed theatre but a new language of the screen.

This new language should be the subtlest and most versatile of all the arts. It has the capacity to present the very essence of a human being. Beyond acting and seeming there is a mysterious reality which, now and then, we catch a glimpse of, and which the camera can be ever on the alert to record. This hidden 'being' of the person should be the real quarry of the cinematographer. It is there in all of us, but rarely seen, except when sometimes revealed by an involuntary gesture, a ripple from the unconscious, which the camera can capture if ready and not distracted. The director prepares the scene for this revelation and then awaits the epiphany. All other considerations are unworthy of this art-form now at our disposal. Until this century we had only succeeded in producing some cumbersome art forms to capture this mystery. Now we at last have an art-form capable of tracking something of this mercurial essence, whether in a glance or a gesture, or a movement of the face.

Such possibility made Bresson himself vow "not to shoot a film in order to illustrate a thesis, or to display men and women confined to their external aspect, but to discover what they are made of, to attain that 'heart of the heart' which does not let itself be caught either by poetry, or by philosophy or by drama" [NC p. 20]. This 'heart of the heart' always remains hidden wherever you have a conscious project on the part of either actors or scriptwriters. The image in a Bresson film must assume the technical humility of an icon which allows something other than the depiction to shine through. His aim is to slow down our frantic ransacking of the image for its narrative content and allow us to gaze at the reality itself: "Against the tactics of speed, of noise, set the tactics of slowness, of silence" [NC p. 28]. Speaking of the fundamental attitude of the cinematographer, he quotes the admonition 'Be attentive' from the Greek Orthodox liturgy, "one must not seek, one must wait"; the purpose of such films is to "make visible what, without you, might never have been seen" [NC p. 39].

LEAN MYTHOLOGY

The neat categories of arthouse movies and commercial cinema need not always apply. There are exceptions. Sometimes the most artistic films became blockbusters on the commercial screen. One such director who covered himself with glory in both vernaculars was David Lean (March 25th, 1908 – April 16th, 1991). He was an English film director, producer, screenwriter and editor, responsible for large-scale epics such as *The Bridge on the River Kwai* (1957), *Lawrence of Arabia* (1962), and *Dr Zhivago* (1965). Earlier in his career he adapted Dickens' novels *Great Expectations* (1946) and *Oliver Twist* (1948) as well as directing the romantic drama *Brief Encounter* (1945) based on the 1936 stage play by Noel Coward, *Still Life*. Lean's body of work in the film industry spanned the period from 1930 to 1984. Many of his films gained critical acclaim from the arthouse as well as grossing huge profits for the industry. He is the only British director to receive two Oscars for his direction and as of 2015, his film *Dr Zhivago* is the eighth highest-grossing movie of all time. Like Dickens in the 19th Century, Lean was a great storyteller in the medium of the 20th Century. His films are based on historical reality but they expand, in his treatment, to mythological proportions. *Lawrence of Arabia* uses the life of a recognised and famous historical figure to tell the story of everyone and anyone faced with a journey through the desert.

Notwithstanding the stellar list of actors involved, the desert is the main character in the film and the Super Panavision 70 cinematography of Freddie Young does justice to the subject. And when we say that Lean builds the story to the level of myth, we are suggesting that such events have always happened and continue to happen in every country and culture around the word and that they assume the status of a universal archetype where particular local and historical details are subsumed into the bigger picture of universal shape and form. As we have seen probably the most ancient and most famous account of such encounters with the desert is the exodus story in the Bible. Even here facts and events which may have had natural causes are invested with mythological significance. For instance, the crossing of the Red Sea and the feeding of the multitude of Israelites can be read in either fashion.

When the dew lifted from the desert they saw "a thing delicate powdery as fine hoarfrost" on the ground, and they said to one another: "What is that?" "That," said Moses, "is the bread the Lord gives you to eat!" They were puzzled and disappointed. They called it 'Man-hu' which means 'What is that?' God never told them what it was, except that this mysterious thing was to be their desert food – their *viaticum* (food for the way) – until they reached the Promised Land.

It was like coriander seed, white in colour, and resembled wafers made with honey. Commentators say that manna and the quails were a 'natural' event. Quails migrate across the desert from North Africa to Southern Europe. Manna, they say, is a secretion from insects which live in tamarisk trees. This may be. But the manna recorded here has mysterious properties. Even though some gathered more, and some less, everyone had as much as they needed; if anyone collected more than they needed for the day, it deteriorated and bred maggots so it could not be used on the following day. On the sixth day they could gather a double portion, enough to last for the Sabbath, and this portion did not deteriorate or breed maggots; the manna ceased on the day they set foot in the Promised Land (Joshua 5:12). It was eventually preserved successfully in a jar which was later put into the Ark of the Covenant with the tablets of stone, to remind the people of God's wonderful intervention on their behalf in the desert.

Manna typifies the spiritual nourishment essential for successful journeying through the wilderness. Jesus claims to be its fulfilment: "I am the bread of life" (John 6:35). "It was not Moses who gave you bread from heaven, it was my father, and this bread gives life to the world"

(John 6:33). Manna remained a mystery to the pilgrims in the desert. It was several hundred years later, with the full realisation of what manna really was, that they wrote in the Book of Wisdom (16: 20-21): "You gave them the food of angels, from heaven untiringly sending them bread already prepared, containing every delight, satisfying every taste. And the substance you gave demonstrated your tenderness towards your children, for, conforming to the taste of whoever ate it, it transformed itself into what each eater wished."[55]

As for the great event of the Israelite crossing of the Red Sea, we do not know where the pursuers caught up with the fugitives, whether in the neighbourhood of the present Suez or further north at one of the bitter lakes or at the gulf of Aqaba. (The Battle of Aqaba on July 6th, 1917 is one of the big moments in Lean's film, though his depiction of a sweeping charge by the Arabs against the town, historians tell us, is quite false. The defences of Aqaba are also exaggerated in the film, with a pair of 12-inch cannons pointing out to sea to prevent naval attack.) As for the crossing of the Red Sea, wherever it may have happened, a natural process, or a series of natural processes (whether a combination of tides with unusual winds which raised them tremendously, or the effect of distant volcanic phenomena on the movement of the sea) could explain what happened. This combined with a daring advance on the part of the Israelites and a destruction of the Egyptians, whose heavy war chariots are caught in the sand or the swamp, leads to the saving of the one and the downfall of the other.

What is decisive with respect to the mythological dimension of these events is that they are understood as an act of God, as a 'miracle'.

The concept of miracle is part of mythology. Miracle need not be something 'supernatural' or 'superhistorical,' but an incident, an event, which can be fully included in the objective, scientific nexus of nature and history. However, its vital meaning explodes the fixity of the fields

55 Frances Hogan, *Words of Life from Exodus*, London, 1984, pp. 146-148.

of experience named 'Nature' and 'History'. Irrelevant whether 'much' or 'little,' unusual things or usual, tremendous or trifling events happened; what is vital is only that what happened was experienced, while it happened, as the act of God.[56]

Most people fail to recognise the shift in register that characterise the films of David Lean. His film *Lawrence of Arabia* for instance, is viewed as an historical documentary rather than as a mythological epic. The hero of this film is an Everyman journeying through the desert rather than any particular human being who actually existed in recent history. Many complaints about the film's accuracy concerned the characterisation of Lawrence himself. The film depicts him as an egotist, and the degree to which Lawrence sought or shunned attention is vigorously debated. Lowell Thomas, who wrote *With Lawrence in Arabia* said that he could take pictures of him only by tricking him, although he also commented that Lawrence "had a genius for backing into the limelight". This last remark referred to the fact that the extraordinary actions that Lawrence accomplished prevented him from being as private as he would have liked. And that is the important point. What Lawrence achieved in historical reality allowed him to be hoisted to another dimension in the idiom of myth. The most vehement critic of the film's accuracy was the protagonist's younger brother and literary executor, Arnold Lawrence, who had sold the rights to his brother's autobiography *Seven Pillars of Wisdom* to Lean for £25,000.

Arnold went on a campaign in the United States and Britain denouncing the film, which he called "a psychological recipe". "Take an ounce of narcissism, a pound of exhibitionism, a pint of sadism, a gallon of blood-lust and a sprinkle of other aberrations and stir well." The perceived problems with the portrayal begin with the differences in physical appearance: the 6ft 2in (1.88 m) Peter O'Toole being almost

---

56 Martin Buber, *Moses: The Revelation and the Covenant*, Harper Torchbooks, New York, 1958, pp. 75-77.

nine inches (23 cm) taller than the 5ft 5in (1.65 m) T.E. Lawrence. Noel Coward quipped after seeing the première of the film, "If you had been any prettier, the film would have been called Florence of Arabia." The criticisms were not restricted to Lawrence. The Allenby family lodged a formal complaint against Columbia about the portrayal of him. Descendants of Auda abu Tayi and the real Sherif Ali went further, suing Columbia despite the fact that the film's Ali was recognisably fictional. The Auda case went on for almost ten years before it was dropped.

A similar misunderstanding led Lean's 1970 film *Ryan's Daughter* to excoriation in Ireland and critical condemnation in many quarters. The film, set in Ireland from August 1917 - January 1918, tells the story of a married Irish woman who has an affair with a British officer during the First World War. It was a box office success, grossing nearly $31 million on a budget of $13.3 million, and won two Academy Awards. Despite the fact that the script, written by Robert Bolt and David Lean, was based on Flaubert's *Madame Bovary* and therefore only quite accidentally situated in Ireland, it gave offence to many Irish people. Some criticised it as an attempt to blacken the legacy of the 1916 Easter Rising and the subsequent Irish War of Independence, especially in relation to the eruption of 'the Troubles' in Northern Ireland around the time of the film's release. It received the following notice in The National Film Institute's report: "When for the production of this film Lean sought period German weapons from the Irish Army authorities, he bolstered his request with a letter from a retired army colonel to the effect that there was nothing in the script to portray the Irish in an unfavourable light... The portrayal of the village idiot by Mills is as disgusting and as nauseating as his acting is excellent. The part played by Sarah Miles - the local publican's daughter - the village beauty, shows the Irish country girls in a disgustingly immoral light... A film with little theme, with little regard for the true situation of the 1916 period."

Lean took these criticisms very seriously and personally, claiming at the time that he would never make another film. This led him to take a 14-year break from filmmaking, during which he planned a number of film projects which never came to fruition. In 1984 he had a career revival with *A Passage to India* which proved to be the last film Lean would direct. And this is the film which best illustrates the point I am trying to make.

The story mostly concerns the trial of a young Indian doctor for the rape of a young woman visiting India for the first time. E.M. Forster did not want his novel to be made into a film. David Lean was determined to do so ever since he read the book. He had to wait until 1984 to carry out this intention. Forster acknowledges that his novel was understood by the critic Peter Burra who wrote of it: "he uses buildings and places and the names of places – such places as can be appropriately associated with a recurring idea, and thus take on significance as symbols – to be the framework of his books... The Marabar caves are the basis of a tour de force in literary planning. They are the keynote in the symphony to which the strange melody always returns. During the first half of the book constant reference to them directs attention forward to the catastrophe. After this, every reference to them directs our attention back to the centre, to the mystery which is never solved."

For both Forster and Lean, India represents a place, a reality, for which the actual geographical country is a symbol. All through the story, visitors keep asking to see the real India. The real India is closed to both the British Raj and most of the Indians themselves. Both have become caricatures made in the likeness of the other: oppressor and oppressed. 'The real India' is not a place, it is the experience of a reality inside ourselves, beyond the everyday reality we experience in India or anywhere else. In both the film and the novel, the Marabar caves are the external shape of such a reality. These are hollowed out spaces within the mountain range, honeycombed with such bubbles. "The caves are easily described," Forster tells us, "a tunnel eight feet long, five feet high, three feet wide, leads to a circular chamber about 20 feet in diameter. This arrangement occurs again and again throughout the group of hills, and this is all, this is a Marabar cave. Having seen one such cave, having seen two, having seen three, four, 14, 24, the visitor returns uncertain whether he has had an interesting experience or a dull one or any experience at all." [124][57]

The experience that Adela Quested underwent in the Marabar caves was of an otherness which caused a kind of ecstasy which only poetry or music might touch upon because it cannot be put into words. It is an experience of nothing. Nothing happened in the cave. "Nothing, nothing attaches to them, and their reputation – for they have one – does not depend upon human speech . . . They are dark caves. There is little to see, and no eye to see it, until the visitor arrives for his five minutes, and strikes a match. Immediately another flame arises in the depths of the rock and moves towards the surface like an imprisoned spirit . . . A bubble-shaped cave that has neither ceiling nor floor, and mirrors its own darkness in every direction infinitely." [125]

In the experience of most, such ecstasy can find analogous expression only in a sexual metaphor. In the film it is made clear to us that *A Passage to India* takes place in one of these caves. The passage, or tunnel, between Adela and the entrance to the cave is clearly depicted as such a metaphor. She is inside and we are with her looking out. Dr Aziz, who is searching for her, is shown at the entrance to the cave looking more like a spider or a pygmy than a man. The scale of the passageway is shown clearly to be beyond the scope of any human person to penetrate. Later there is a pan of Aziz running down the mountainside like a fly moving across the back of an elephant. He is being moved by forces larger than any his own inner motivation could supply. The 'real India' has erupted and he just happens to be caught along the side of the volcano. Adela has most certainly been raped, but not by Aziz or any human agent.

The law court, which occupies most of the second half of the film,

57 All references to E.M. Forster's *A Passage to India* are taken from the 1962 Penguin edition and the pages are given in square brackets in these paragraphs.

is unable to cope with the situation. Here there is only room for one thing or another: either/or, black or white, yes or no. Did he or did he not? In the end Adela is forced to admit that nothing happened, that her overwhelming experience in the empty cave had nothing to do with Dr Aziz. After all the trouble and the publicity involved in setting up the trial, all those involved are deflated by her eventual refusal to press charges. It is a scandal, an outrage, a disgrace to the Raj and she has removed their opportunity to punish the rebels; she has humiliated the Raj by her pusillanimity and she has taken the whole of India for a ride. But what both the film and the novel are trying to explain, in ways far more subtle than the language of law, is that India has indeed taken her for a ride and she has undergone the most cataclysmic event possible. Nothing did happen to Miss Quested, and the experience was so overwhelming that it changed her life completely. For this experience, she later wrote to Aziz, 'I owe to India a debt which I shall never repay in person.'

The transformation which occurred in her was recognised by Fielding, another English character in the novel, and it gave him "a new-born respect" for Miss Quested because "although her hard school-mistressy manner remained, she was no longer examining life, but being examined by it; she had become a real person". [238] And Fielding also knew that such an event in the Marabar caves had passed him by "with averted face and on swift wings".

> He experienced nothing himself; it was as if someone had told him there was such a moment and he was obliged to believe. And he felt dubious and disconcerted suddenly, and wondered whether he was really and truly successful as a human being – after 40 years' experience he had learnt to manage his life and make the best of it on advanced European lines, had developed his personality, explored his limitations, controlled his passions – and he had done it all without becoming either pedantic or worldly. A creditable achievement, but as the moment passed, he felt he ought to have

been working at something else the whole time – he didn't know at what, never would know, never could know, and that was why he felt sad. [187]

What had happened to Adela inside the caves? The first half of Lean's film is a ride with Mrs Moore and Miss Quested on the back of an elephant up to the caves in search of the real India. The second half of the film tries to find out what happened when they got there, using one of the more established methods for eking out the truth which is a court of law. The real question being asked is: what exactly are the Marabar caves? "What miscreant lurked in them, presently to be detected by the activities of the law? Who was the guide, and had he been found yet? What was the 'echo' of which the girl complained? He did not know, but presently he would know. Great is information, and she shall prevail." [187] Information does not prevail, especially if we continue to view India "as in a frieze" and fail "to grasp it as a spirit". We are driven back to the central moment of the film and the novel where "the small black hole gaped" and we "were sucked in like water down a drain". [144] Law is inadequate to the task of revealing this mystery.

David Lean presents *A Passage* as a mystery of an empty tomb, another kind of passage, a paschal mystery; the irruption into our world of another kind of space and time. Its darkness sets our own re-echoing. The only other witness, now dead, who had refused to attend the trial, described what happened to her as "something very old and very small. Before time, it was before space also. Something snub-nosed, incapable of generosity – the undying worm itself". The Marabar caves are small round cavities hollowed into the granite of a mountain range. Nobody knows how many there are but it is supposed that the whole range is honeycombed. "Certain chambers have no entrances, chambers never unsealed since the arrival of the Gods," exceeding in number "those that can be visited as the dead exceed the living – four hundred of them, four thousand or million". Only some have been broken into; the others are surmised by the hollow-sounding echo which reverberates in the cup of each individual cavern. The audience of every showing of this film form such a mountain range of interior caverns. The film lights a match in this darkness which can "allow another flame to arise out of the depths of the rock and move towards the surface like an imprisoned spirit".

PART IV

CHRISTIANITY AS MYSTERY

The milieu in which Christianity took form was one quite familiar with mystery religions. The cults of Eleusis, Dionysius, Attis, Isis and Mithras for example offered their devotees, their initiates (*mystes*), salvation (*soteria*) by dispensing cosmic life through various sacramental actions that allowed for essential change through participation with the deity. These mystery religions comprised both cultic actions such as meals, fertility rites, baptisms, investitures and symbolic journeys, and they involved hidden teachings, an arcane secret tradition with regard to which the initiates took vows of silence. Such secret knowledge differentiated them from outsiders.

Gnosticism was one of the first heresies with which Christianity had to contend, and from which it had to differentiate itself. It is understandable that every attempt was made to rid the newly established mystery religion of all connection with any ambiguous terminology redolent of the circumambient cults that threatened to invade, dilute or dissipate the originality that Christianity incorporated into its liturgy and sacraments. However, the bitterness and intensity of the struggle between Gnosticism and early Christianity was owing to their proximity rather than their difference; it was caused by the similarity that threatened to absorb, rather than any heterogeneity that might define them as contradictory opposites.

Whatever the dangers of misinterpretation or of identification with alien religions, Christianity remains essentially a mystery religion. And this means that its substance, its secret core, can never become comprehensively enshrined in any work of human hands of whatever variety or intricacy.

Scripture as well as tradition speak of the mysteries of Jesus Christ in the singular and the plural. St Paul uses much of the terminology of a mystery religion when introducing his converts to the essence of Christianity. He speaks of "the mystery of God" (Col 2:2) and "the 'mystery of Christ" (Col 4:3; Eph 3:4). This Mystery is the work of salvation, the fulfilment of humankind and thereby of all creation. "It is decisively bound up with the name, person, life, mystery, death, and resurrection of Jesus Christ and their effective prolongation in the event of the Church."[58] For St Paul and for the whole New Testament, as well as for the authentic tradition of the Church, Christianity is the revelation of the Mystery. *Mysterion*, the mystery, is the eternal counsel (wisdom, *sophia*) hidden in God (Eph, 3:9) before ever the world came to be (1 Cor 2:7) whose eventual manifestation will mean the end of this world (Eph, 1:10). The context of the Mystery is 'salvation history' wherein the two components, salvation and history combine.

> Salvation is simultaneously immanent and transcendent vis-à-vis history. Similarly, the Mystery unfolds and differentiates itself in the mysteries; it needs them, but without exhausting itself in them. The mysteries lend the Mystery vividness, tangibility, concreteness, reality, and efficacy. On the other hand, the Mystery endows the mysteries with something of its presence, wholeness, fullness, and reality, so that in them one touches the Mystery itself.[59]

The apostolic mission is part of the unfolding of this mystery (Eph 3:2,9) and Paul himself as steward of the mystery must be acquainted with these secrets, the gift of a prophet being to penetrate the mysteries of God (1 Cor 2:10; 4:1; 13:2) and become acquainted with all the mysteries.

Mysterion (the hidden mystery) is connected with *Kerygma* (the proclaimed message) as the Father is manifested by the Son, who is an

---

58 Christian Schultz, O.S.B., 'The Mysteries of the Life of Jesus as a Prism of Faith,' *Communio* 29 (Spring 2002) p. 30.
59 Ibid. p. 30.

epistle (from the Greek *epi* + *stellein*, meaning 'to send') from God. All knowledge of God is a mystery both in the way it is communicated and the way it is received. No human agency has proprietary claims, production control, or distribution rights in this regard. The way a mystery is handed on is itself a mystery.

Tradition in the early Church was a fund of unwritten customs and mysteries making up the sacramental and religious life of the community (*ta agrapha tes ekklesesias mysteria*) necessary for understanding the truth of revelation and pointing to the mysterial character of Christian knowledge as a gnosis of God (*gnosis theou*) which is a gift conferred through such traditions.

Later, very much later, this oral tradition was written down and eventually hammered into dogmas and creedal formulae, which became the *breviatum verbum* (the abridged version), as John Cassian[60] calls the Symbol of Antioch, making allusion to St Paul in Rom 9:27, who in turn is alluding to Isaiah 10:22. It was in the 4th Century that the preferred rendering of the Greek term for mystery became 'sacrament' which referred most especially to Baptism and the Eucharist.

In the Pauline understanding, an essential element of the Mystery of God, and thus of Christ, is its cultic celebration. It is, in a very significant sense, a 'mystery of cult'. The Mystery almost automatically gives birth to cult; the cultic dimension in its turn continually points back to the foundation and content of the Mystery. The celebration of the Mystery unfolds in rites and symbols. At its core, the celebration revolves around the mystery of the death and resurrection of the Lord, whose remembrance is observed each week as well as annually at Easter. That the Christian cultic mystery is 'paschal' expresses the core of the mystery as such.[61]

....

60 John Cassian *De Incarnatione* VI, 3. Cf also St Augustine *De Symbolo* 1; St Cyril of Jerusalem, *Catechesis* V, 12.

61 Christian Schultz, O.S.B., 'The Mysteries of the Life of Jesus as a Prism of Faith,' *Communio* 29 (Spring 2002) p. 36.

However, Christ does not call us to a new cult which would be estranged from the normal rhythm of our lives, a new ritual gesture, a new devotion, a new prayer-machine. Christ calls us to life. "I came that they may have life and have it to the full" (John 10:10). Christianity is not a new religion, in some narrow sense; it is a new form of existence. Our expression of that new form of existence is a new song, is praise. We are swept up into the love of God. Again, this phrase 'swept up' is not just rhetorical. It describes a new form of ecstatic existence which is for real. God's love is contagious. But we must allow ourselves to be touched by it constantly to catch the fever. Sacramental life provides those touchstones. This is what 'doing' theology means. Anything less becomes 'heresy' which word means 'cutting yourself away,' cutting off the branch that holds you in place, cutting off your nose to spite your face.

The Christian is called forth (*Ecclesia*) by God to real freedom, real joy, real life, which are only possible in and through relationship with the only society of perfect love: the three persons in one God, the Trinity of perfectly equal and reciprocated relationship. Revelation of the Trinity is revelation to us of the meaning of 'person' as a reality, and the meaning of 'love,' as a way of life.

These are not realities we can understand intellectually; they are realities which have to be done with the full reality of our total person and our whole life. Such is love as generosity, love out of plenitude not need, love as outgoing and self-giving, an overflow of fullness. Prayer is allowing the life of the Trinity to circulate in our hearts. It is breathing the Spirit. We embody this love in such a way that it transforms us and we become its icons. The Spirit is the artist who moulds us into our most satisfying and appropriate shape which is in the image and likeness of God.

The Incarnation of Jesus Christ is the perfect translation of this love into human form. This is what is meant by saying 'the word was made flesh'. This flesh became word again in the written text of the Bible. Exegesis of Scripture means living it with our whole person for our whole life. Without encountering the details or weighing up the practicability, we are still aware that at the very least this must involve right relationships in every sphere. Everything that promotes fullness of humanity furthers this cause. The second person of the Trinity became one of us to show what we really are and what we are capable of becoming. Christ became human to show us that real existence is quite different from what we had imagined. His life was a counter-witness to prevailing interpretations of the word 'life' and it continues to be so.

The glory of God, as St Irenaeus has put it so succinctly, is any one of us fully alive, and 'orthodoxy' as the word tells us in Greek is 'the right way' to glorify God. Essential to that task is establishing real and lasting, indeed everlasting, contact with the living God. The ecstasy of God meets the ecstasy of human beings and creates a new form of existence.

This is not just rhetorical gymnastics. As persons, we are ecstatic. 'Existence' means to stand outside ourselves (*ex-sistere*). By nature our person is biologically incarnate in one limited, individual substance. Through love we can escape from that imprisonment in ecstatic transport towards another. *Amor transit in conditionem objecti*, a Medieval maxim, means that love takes on the identity of the loved one. Eros is our self-transcendence, our going beyond the limits of our individual prison to communion with another.

Each of us is the product of love between two people. Persons create other persons through love. So the person in itself is capable of self-transcendence, self-perpetuation.

What happens in the new form of life which God has allowed us to share is that our person becomes inserted into God's nature. This is what is meant by being adopted children of God. We cannot become such children naturally and so it has been arranged that we be so by adoption. The ecstasy of our love can thereby become everlasting. The natural life of our bodily existence, when grafted to the body of Christ, is regenerated by an eternal energy which allows us to transcend the boundaries of our naturally limited personhood. The link between these two forms of personal life (ours and God's) is necessarily artificial, like an iron lung or a plastic limb; it is a new form of existence which we call 'ecclesial' (those who have been called out of their natural, biological, bodily individuality). Liturgy is the technology devised to effect and perpetuate this link.

Orthodoxy (the right way of giving praise) moves our relationship beyond manipulation, using God or anyone else for our own purposes. The possibilities we usually hope for are of our own invention, and we use worship to blackmail God, to force God's hand; we try to lure God into becoming implicated in our plans. Such religion is worship as politics or investment. True religion moves us beyond idolatry, worshipping whatever or whoever enslaves us, holds us in thrall; beyond ideology, propaganda of whatever kind for whatever politics.

Worship as it should be is praise as an attitude of openness and total trust in the future which God has in mind for our attention and cooperation. We should not mortgage this future for what we want of the present. Instead we should be attentive to the slightest hint, perhaps only a whisper, undeveloped and unformed, coming from the Spirit. As we follow this hunch, what at first seems barely a whisper, eventually becomes audible and pivotal as a directive towards, or a burgeoning of, a quite different future to any we had ever imagined. We have no idea what life beyond the natural limitations of our being might look like, we have to be tutored in this as we have to be trained to walk the path of resurrection.

Such participation in the determination of a future as yet unimagined is the practical realisation of our frequent prayer 'Thy kingdom come, Thy will be done'. It requires a concentrated orchestration of real presence to the present, to the moment which is the turnstile towards the future. Each present moment is a railroad switch offering possibilities of redirection. 'Religion' says Rilke 'is a natural animation within a being through whom the wind of God blows three times a day, as a consequence of which we are at least - supple.'[62]

....

62 Rainer Maria Rilke, *Selected Letters 1902-1926*, Quartet Books, London, 1998, p. 337.

True worship as praise allows us to open fully as flowers do towards the sunlight, in the direction of the most expansive and fruitful future. Such an exercise is open to the past through inspired *anamnesis*, 'remembering' the wonderful working of God in our own lives in the past, as well as in the evolutionary history of the planet; and is open to the future through *epiclesis* (invocation of the Spirit) which eliminates our own agenda and disposes us towards God's originality. In between the two movements towards past and future, comes the moment of consecration of the present, the platform from where we take our transport. Such 'real presence,' as we call it, is accomplished most fully and completely in the Eucharist (which means 'thanksgiving).

Every relationship requires rites, ceremonies, practical arrangements in time and space, to structure, maintain, fasten and secure its depth and durability. Christian liturgy has been called 'the cult of the Trinity': the way in which we accomplish in our space-time continuum the life of ever-expanding selflessness and sublime generosity, which is the invasion of our being by divine love.

Christianity, as ritual, must be anchored in the time and space of the original event of resurrected life, the moment when Christ as human being passed over from life on this Earth to divine life in Heaven without allowing anything of His humanity to fall away. We are grounded in the real presence of the Risen Lord.

The essential connection between us and Divine life is not established, however, with and through the historical humanity of Jesus Christ as a man who shared our nature; it is established by, with and through His person. As person He is one of the Trinity of persons, He is self-giving communion with the other two persons, He is God as love. But, also as person, He is human and is in communion with each one of us to the extent that we realise this and live it with everything we have and are. Such is the essential business of Christianity. It is the business of divine love. Anything other than that, anything that distracts us from this essential relationship is leading us astray.

The Church and the Eucharist which establish the life of Christianity are instituted by Christ but constituted by the Holy Spirit.

Baptism, the Eucharist, the ecclesial community, establish our communion with the persons of the Trinity, energise our lives from eternity, burst through our space-time capsule and insert the oxygen of infinity, not just as an addition to, or a substitute for, our natural being, but as a transplant, a new creation, a relational metaphysics, a being as communion. What takes place is as miraculous and as revitalising as a heart transplant. Each one of us becomes energised by the heart of God.

The self-emptying of our being as an autonomous, self-possessed, lonely individual substance, to allow for this transplant and the consequent harnessing of our human source of love to the infinite divine one, is the necessary preparation. Egotistical me can allow myself to be corroded by the quicklime of the Eucharist. In so doing, I become what I already am by baptism, an adopted member of this community of love. "All our lives are the moment of Baptism," St Basil says. He means that it takes us that long to catch up with ourselves, to grow into the reality we have become by that mystery; growing into the reality of our new being, our everlasting life, our universal and eternal communion. We burst our being to get beyond it towards a new existence of love.

MYTH-MAKING LITURGY

The strange but important truth is that God's presence can never be immediately transparent, uncomplicatedly available. God has to be God and we have to be ourselves and never the twain shall meet in the same time-space dimension, because this very dimension had to be invented so that we could stand on our own two feet without being reabsorbed into God. So this barrier is our only safeguard as human beings. And it means in turn that we cannot know God directly: there is, there has to be, a secret wisdom, which subverts our natural capacity to know, which is constitutionally incapable of direct vision of God.

We have to know in the way we were made, in the way that we are. This is because we were born with a mind and there is nothing we can do about it. The mind came with the body, they go as a set. And this mind-set requires that if we want to 'know' God we have to learn and develop a secret wisdom that goes against the grain of natural knowledge. This secret wisdom is about the presence of God in our world, which cannot be other than secret. If it were manifest it would be so obvious that there would be no freedom on our part to know or love God. Our freedom demands that any knowledge of the God who made us must be hidden in the world God made. Like an expert thief God had to steal himself away without leaving any obvious clues behind which would identify the world as his manufacture.

So, the reason why knowledge of God is hidden is because our minds are otherwise focused, our interest is elsewhere, and our education trains us to overlook it. We are fashioned like the detectives in a story by Edgar Allen Poe called 'The Purloined Letter'. We search the house and every room, in all the places we have learnt to search for hidden items: under the carpet, inside the panels of drawers, behind the skirting of the floor boards, behind picture frames, unscrewing legs of chairs to examine spaces between these, tapping on walls to locate hollow crevices, when all the time the letter escaped our notice in a letter rack on the mantelpiece. The presence of God in our world is so obvious that we fail to notice it, just as we completely ignore the watches on our wrists, don't even know we have one on, until we need it to tell us a certain kind of time. The truth is that we are too clever by half to recognise the obvious. Our minds are oblivious to it, as they are to the glasses on our noses or contact lenses in our eyes, which allow some of us to see.

"The Church's *leitourgia*, a term much more comprehensive and adequate than 'worship' or 'cult,' is the full 'epiphany' – expression, manifestation, fulfilment of that in which the Church believes, or what constitutes her faith." I am using the words of Alexander Schmemann (1921-1983), Russian Orthodox liturgical theologian. All initiation to, explanation of, integration into the mystery of Christianity is 'mystagogical,' which means that these can only be accomplished through these mysteries themselves. It is the mysteries themselves. Christian mysteries alone can show us what they are in themselves. So, Schmemann sees liturgy "as the *locus theologicus* par excellence because it is its very function, its *leitourgia* in the original meaning of that word, to manifest and to fulfil the Church's faith, and to manifest it not partially, not 'discursively,' but as living totality and catholic experience."

Every liturgy is, in a certain way, a celebration of the Epiphany, the 'manifestation' of God to God's people. Liturgy is where such manifestation happens. It is the technology for replaying the mystery. For St John, the Incarnation and the whole of Christ's life is presented as an epiphany. Christianity is a mystery of epiphany. The mystery reveals itself through the mysteries. The mystery takes place in our world in real time liturgically.

Liturgy invokes poetic licence when dealing with the mystery which inspires it. In the monastic antiphonary there is a kaleidoscopic mixture of imagery which proclaims at Vespers on the feast of the Epiphany: "Three great wonders fell on this day: Today the star guided the Wise Men to the

Child in the crib. Today water became wine at the wedding feast. Today Christ our salvation was baptised in the Jordan.'[63] This threefold 'today' as Peter Henrici points out,[64] is somewhat confusing since it encompasses a period of thirty years and does not even reflect any actual chronology of events. The corresponding antiphon from Lauds of the same feast of the Epiphany adds to the confusion: "Today the Church was wedded to the heavenly bridegroom. In the Jordan, Christ washed her clean of her sins. The Wise Men hurry with gifts to the wedding of the king. Water is transformed into wine and gladdens the guests"[65]

Whatever about the chronology or the characters involved, the liturgy here is celebrating nothing less than a marriage between Heaven and Earth, "the eschatological nuptial mystery", the love of God for us. Liturgy describes this in a fireworks display of imagery, in a love-poem about a wedding-feast.

The reconstruction we weave with our liturgy is designed from the template laid down by Jesus Christ in the 33 years during which He lived on this Earth. His arrival marks a starting point. So in the West, we mark time as B.C. or A.D. Those letters mean nothing until referenced to the primal story of Western Christendom, the Story of Jesus Christ. Every day of His life acts as a station, a *Gestalt*, in the unfolding of His biography, and as a template for the future unfolding of human history, if we allow ourselves to follow in His footsteps. Liturgy is the vernacular we use for the ritualistic retelling of His Story. It offers the possibility of His Story becoming the equivalent of our history. And the story has been carefully orchestrated liturgically with the great celebrations of Christmas, Easter and Pentecost, as punctuation marking that time.

....

63 Tribus miraculis ornatum diem sanctum colimus: hodie stella Magos duxit ad praesepium: hodie vinum ex aqua factum est ad nuptias: hodie in Jordane a Joanne Christus baptizari voluit, ut salvaret nos, alleluia.

64 Peter Henrici 'The Miracle of Cana' in *Communio*, Spring 2006, pp. 5-10.

65 Hodie caelesti sponso juncta est Ecclesia, quoniam in Jordane lavit Christus ejus crimina: currunt cum muneribus Magi ad regales nuptias, et ex aqua facto vino laetantur convivae, alleluia.

The light of the sun which we cannot see breaks into visible components which we can see as it appears on Earth. Using a prism to refract or break the invisible light we can watch its separation into a visible spectrum of violet, blue, green, yellow, orange and red. In a similar way our 'mysteries' refract the light of 'the mystery' and allow it to unfold before our eyes. Our liturgy performs a similar refraction of the life of God on Earth by dividing the temporal year we pass through annually into a spectrum of purple, green, pink, white, gold and red as we celebrate the moments of Christ's life from His coming in Advent to His birth at Christmas to His Epiphany and His Baptism; then we change to purple for His journey through the desert in Lent, His suffering and death at Passiontide, His rising from the dead at Easter, His ascension into Heaven and His sending of the Holy Spirit at Pentecost. And the cloth we weave is a cloth of gold because there are divine threads running through it to make up one seamless garment of Incarnation, following the red thread of His every action, gesture, movement while here on Earth. Liturgy is a cloth of gold, a many-splendoured dream coat, woven like a cobweb between the fingertips of the human and the divine. Scarlet and gold are the colours of the cloak of salvation. The technology, the art, which human beings use to connect with the divine is the symbolism of worship or liturgy. Through it we are holding open a matrix of possibility. The liturgy enacts a different world. It sings the song of a world that is open to possibility. It uses symbols that are avatars of openness. Victor Turner defines a symbol as a 'storage unit,' the basic 'molecule' of ritual activity. Ritual symbols are seen as 'multi-vocal,' they never have one specific never-changing meaning. They may represent many things at the one time. Multivocality endows ceremonies, even those of the simplest form, with multiple layers of meaning.

Since Jesus Christ arrived on our planet over 2,000 years ago the world we live in has been perforated. His resurrection blew a hole through the roof of the space-time continuum that makes up our earthly habitat. From that moment onwards we are asked to take out dual citizenship between time and eternity. We have become rooted in *both* realms. "There is no difference in the Lord's sight between one day and a thousand years; to Him, the two are the same." (2 Peter 3:8b-9) The time and space we are invited to cohabit is the 'now' of resurrected time. This does not describe any chronological duration of time but is "a qualitative change in how time is experienced". It is the 'kairos' time of the kingdom that Jesus came to inaugurate. This breath from elsewhere, which is the Holy Spirit, maintains at all moments the possibility of intimations from that other world where the three persons of the Trinity conduct their loving existence together.

The liturgy is not a book that we read, a ceremony that we perform, an illustration of some principle that we believe in; it is a deed that we do that makes present the time and space of God's redeeming act, the rescue operation, involving the three Persons of the Trinity, here and now. And this Mystery, in the predominantly Pauline sense, "means, first of all, a deed of God's, the working-out of an eternal divine plan through an act which proceeds from His eternity, is realised in time and the world, and returns once more to Him, its goal in eternity". "And it is because liturgy is that living totality and that catholic experience by the Church of her own faith that it is the very *source* of theology, the condition that makes both the Church and theology *possible*. For theology is not a mere sequence of more or less individual interpretations of this or that 'doctrine' in the light and thought forms of this or that 'culture' and 'situation,' but rather the attempt to express Truth itself, to find words adequate to the mind and experience of the Church, which is precisely the function of the *leitourgia*."[66]

If God came on Earth to reveal to us the mystery of what it means to be fully human, this truth cannot be contained in formulae, catechisms, books of instruction. This mystery is transmitted liturgically. The Divine

---

66 *Liturgy and Tradition, Theological Reflections of Alexander Schmemann*, ed. Thomas Fisch, St Vladimir's Seminary Press, New York, 1990, pp. 39-40.

love of the Trinity to which we are invited, displays itself in our world, through an idiom which is, at first sight, somewhat esoteric and alienating. In order to prevent itself from being cheapened, from being less than it was intended to be, it stands on ceremony.

This work of liturgical prayer is not just teaching those who participate the meaning of words and things, it is transforming the very people and the things themselves. Most people who explain the liturgy try to picture for us what happens at the other side of the tapestry where Christ sits in glory at the right hand of the Father in the eternal heavenly worship of the Trinity, surrounded by choirs of angels and saints. But we who are still on this Earth have no real capacity to understand or appreciate what happens in this other dimension. We are desperately extending our human and earthly tendrils, hoping to find some meaningful, sensuous, emotional, psychological and human footholds that we can use to climb this wall between ourselves and eternity.

And it is a wall and will always be a wall between us and what lies ahead of, or beyond, our human lives. The wall is both a separation between the created and the uncreated and a means of communication between the two. Christ has unearthed this wall and covered it with His fingerprints so that we can identify His handiwork. Simone Weil used the word *metaxu* in Greek to describe something that separates at the same time as it connects.[67] For her, every separation was also a link. She illustrates this as follows: "Two prisoners whose cells adjoin communicate with each other by knocking on the wall. The wall is the thing which separates them but it is also their means of communication."

Liturgy is both a barrier and a 'way through' to the 'other' world. The physical world, with everything in it, serves the same purpose as a blind person's stick. Anything here can be used to tap out our relationship with God. The stick does not give direct insight but is used to bring us into practical contact with a reality that is otherwise obscured. So, the liturgy

---

67 This was again in Fanny Howe's essay in *A God in the House,* p. 109.

is the brail we have devised to allow us, who are blind, deaf and dumb in the world of the Spirit, to achieve contact. "Jerusalem is built as a city" the psalm tells us. It is an image or a symbol of the place where God can dwell on Earth. We create this city, this place, these walls, by *doing* liturgy.

For this development of my understanding I am mostly indebted to the fact that I have lived over 50 of my 75 years in a Benedictine monastery. The basic structure of this existence is liturgical. Our Rule dates back to the 6th Century and prescribes a rhythm of life which celebrates on a daily basis the ritualistic enactment of God's life on Earth. This last phrase can have two meanings: it can mean that liturgical action translates the Divine economy into a human idiom, or it can mean that it strives to emulate human behaviour of God incarnate on Earth. And, in a certain sense, it can be interpreted either way.

Christians believe that when Jesus Christ came on Earth He was God in human form. This meant that His every move, His every action, from the day He was born until the day He died were THE way human beings should lead their lives. Trying to recapture that reality in every detail so that each one could be preserved and contemplated by succeeding generations requires a very particular and effective kind of taxidermy. It is not surprising that the most effective kind of monstrance was selected to encase the jewellery of each moment of His life. These snap-shot cameos became known as 'the mysteries' of the life of Christ. "From the 2nd to the 5th Century a broad stream of Greek mystery religion entered into the Church and transformed simple Biblical Christianity into the mystical sacramentalism that survived in the Byzantine-Russian, and to somewhat less degree in the Roman Church."[68]

If it did survive in the Roman Church it was in great part thanks to the liturgy itself, and in the way this was practised over sixteen centuries by members of the Benedictine order. The monastery in Ireland to which

....

68 Hugo Rahner, 'The Christian Mystery and the Pagan Mysteries,' *The Mysteries, Papers from the Eranos Yearbooks*, Bollingen Series XXX – 2, Pantheon Books, 1955, p. 337.

I belong comes from a monastery in Belgium where an Irish Abbot, Columba Marmion, exercised through his writing an influence on the Catholic world of his time. One of his fundamental intuitions was inherited from a German tradition.

Odo Casel is hardly a household name, nor is it ever likely to be. Not surprising as he was an obscure monk who spent the greater part of his monastic life as chaplain to a community of Benedictine nuns.

Johannes Casel was born at Koblenz, in the German Rhineland, on the September 27th, 1886. Entering the monastery of Maria Laach in the autumn of 1905, he went through the usual stages of monastic initiation, receiving the name Odo, making profession in 1907 and being ordained in 1911. In 1921, he became editor of the *Jahrbuch fur Liturgiewissenschaft* (Yearbook for Liturgical Science), which task he acquitted through 15 imposing volumes until wartime shortage of paper precluded further publication in 1941. The *Jahrbuch* is one of the great monuments to the intellectual revival of German Catholicism between the two world wars. On Holy Saturday 1948, he suffered a stroke after singing the *Lumen Christi* during the Paschal Vigil. He died in the early hours of Easter Sunday, March 28th, at the age of 61.

And yet from this obscure monk issued what Pope Benedict XVI called "perhaps the most fruitful theological idea of the 20th Century".[69] "According to Casel, the true nature of the Christian liturgy was misunderstood so long as it was not seen that the liturgy was in its essence not doctrine but mystery, and that, as such, it stood in a generic relationship to the pagan, Eleusinian, Orphic and Hermetic mystery cults."[70]

It is not a matter of chance that all the New Testament writings were composed in Greek – not translated into Greek; that it was the Greek and Roman cities of the Mediterranean area that quickly allowed Christianity to gain a foothold; that it was in them that Christianity could display its

---

69 Joseph Ratzinger, *Die sakramentale Begründung der christlichen Existenz* (Freising, 1970), 5.

70 Giorgio Agamben & Monica Ferrando, *The Unspeakable Girl, The Myth and Mystery of Kore*, Seagull, London, 2014, p. 30.

greatest successes in numerical terms.[71]

Casel considers the classical mysteries as a kind of preparatory school for Christianity. These had a function to fulfil under divine providence, since they made ready models of thought and concepts that could not be found elsewhere, but were necessary for the development of the doctrine of the sacraments.[72]

Christianity, although borrowing from such ancient and sophisticated religiosity, transformed it accordingly: the mystery and the mysteries which Jesus Christ came to reveal are for everyone and not for an elite and restricted group of cognoscenti; they are available to the poor, the simple, the pure of heart. Yet, they remain mysteries. Of course this did not mean that the mysteries of Christianity could be identified or even compared with any such cults, but following the principle of incarnation it meant that 'the profoundest contemplative experience of the ancient world entered into Christianity, where it was purified and completed. In its ability to assimilate such "heathen" elements, Christianity demonstrated its all-embracing catholicity.'[73]

'*Ganzheitschau*' was one of Casel's favourite words: 'a view of the whole.' Mystery theology or the "doctrine/teaching of the Mystery" (*Mysterientheologie, Mysterienlehre*) are the names given to Casel's thought. Christianity is the revelation of the Mystery. "For Paul, Peter and John, the heart of faith is not the teachings of Christ, not the deeds of his ministry, but the acts by which he saves us." This is Christianity in its full and original meaning as the gospel of God. Not a world-view with a religious backdrop, not a theological system or a moral

....

71   Hans-Josef Klauck, *The Religious Context of Early Christianity, A Guide to Graeco-Roman Religions*, Minnealoplis, Fortress Press, 2003, translated from the German, Die religiöse Umwelt des Urchristenstums, Kohlhammer Studienbücher Theologie, vols 9/1 & 9/2, 1995, 1996, by Brian McNeil, p. 5.

72   Ibid. p. 152.

73   Friedrich Heiler, 'Contemplation in Christian Mysticism', Papers from *The Eranos Yearbooks*, edited by Joseph Campbell, Bollingen Series XXX, Volume 4, Princeton University Press, 1985, pp. 192.

law, "but the mysterium in the Pauline sense, that is God's revelation to humankind through theandric acts, full of life and power" and our saving participation in these.[74]

First of all, the Mystery is God Himself, the thrice-holy, dwelling in inaccessible light. We can see ancient humanity's sense of this primal Mystery in the temples and pyramids that remain as evidence. To Israel God revealed Himself more fully. And so we come to the second sense of Mystery: Christ is the *mysterium* in person. He reveals the invisible God in the flesh. His deeds are 'mysteries' also. "The deeds of His self-abasement, and above all His sacrificial death on the cross, are mysteries, because in them God reveals Himself in a way that goes beyond all human standards of measurement. Above all, though, His resurrection and exaltation are mysteries, because in them divine glory was revealed in the man Jesus, and this in a form that is hidden from the world and only open to believers." This last is a point Casel insists on: mystery is by definition a paradox. It is hidden as well as revealed; only faith can 'see' it and only *gnosis*, Spirit-given knowledge, can penetrate it; it is beyond the grasp of the 'world;' it is given to the Church.

And so we arrive at the third sense of *mysterium*, closely connected with the first two. "We find the person of Christ, His saving deeds and the working of His grace in the mysteries of worship." Mystery in this sense denotes "a sacred ritual action, in which a past redemptive deed is made present in the form of a specific rite; the worshipping community, by accomplishing this sacred rite, participates in the redemptive act and thus obtains salvation." This is why liturgy itself is also called 'mystery, the mystery of worship (*Kultmysterium*). It is a mystery because in it "the divine saving act is present under the veil of symbols". As Christ is the mystery of God present in the 'flesh,' so the sacraments are the mystery of Christ present in a liturgical form.

....

74 I am indebted for much of what I say about Casel's understanding of Mystery to Hugh Gilbert OSB http://www.canonlaw.info/liturgysacraments_casel.htm.

Liturgy is not ritual or pageantry or, as some of Casel's contemporaries believed, a collection of rubrics governing public worship in the Church. It is the place, the presence and the power of the mystery of Christ. The sacraments of the Church invest liturgy with the force of the Mystery. Such 'mystery of worship' is "nothing other than the God-man continuing to act on Earth". "The presence of the Lord in the divine mysteries occupies an intermediate position - a middle stage - between the earthly, historical life of Christ and his glorious life in heaven," between the Ascension and the Parousia. As witness to what he regarded as the deeper and more ancient view, Casel invoked the then Prayer over the Gifts of the 9th Sunday after Pentecost:

> "Grant us, we beg You Lord, that we may frequent these mysteries in a worthy way, for every time we celebrate the commemoration of this sacrifice, the work of our redemption is accomplished (*opus nostrae redemptionis exercetur*)."

The actual saving acts of Christ "are so necessary to the Christian that we cannot be a true Christians if we don't live them after Him and with Him. It is not the teaching of Christ which makes the Christian. It is not even the simple application of his grace. It is total identification with the person of Christ obtained by re-living His life". Such 'total identification' with the life, death and resurrection of Christ is what the liturgy makes possible. There is in every one of the saving deeds of the Lord a substantial element transcending time and space and capable of commemoration and re-presentation in a sacramental way (*in sacramento, in mysterio*), which is the meaning of 'presence in mystery' (*Mysterien-gegenwart*). What happened in the past under the veil of historical event, happens now under the veil of sacramental sign. Celebrations are indeed time-and-space bound, but they bring into time and space something that essentially transcends these. Casel understood this presence in terms of a unified whole. The mystery of worship is found certainly in the Eucharist supremely, but also in the whole array of sacraments and sacramentals.

Also, the Mystery naturally tends towards mysticism. The mystery of Christian worship is the surest source and location of life lived in the mystery. By means of it, the mysteries of Christ's humanity become the mysteries of our own. By means of it, the Holy Spirit imparts to believers the true gnosis, an experiential knowledge of the mystery of Christ, taking them beyond the merely rational and into a life of the Trinity. The 'end' of Casel's Mystery Theology points in the same direction as the end of the Rule of St Benedict: "you, whoever you are, who hasten towards your heavenly home, fulfil first of all by the help of Christ this little Rule for beginners. And at length then, under God's protection, you will reach those loftier heights of wisdom and virtue."[75]

The foundation and centre of Christian worship lies in the act of making Jesus Christ present in life, in death, and in resurrection. This 'making present' comes about by means of a living memory, more precisely, the ur-biblical category of 'remembrance' (Latin: *Memoria*, Greek: *anamnesis*), whose essential and proper setting is within cult. The continually renewed gathering of the Christian community for the celebration of the Paschal Mystery, every Christian act of worship, and all forms of liturgy become the medium through which the saving presence of Jesus Christ occurs in an ever new and creative way.[76]

Christianity has devised an alternative year, symbolising a different way of living time, which provides those of us who choose to be otherwise, with a liturgical calendar. We insert the mysteries of Christ's life into the seasons and the times of the year, beginning with Advent and carrying on to Pentecost, from November to June approximately. This allows us to live these mysteries in ways that give access to the full

....

75 Rule Of Benedict Chapter 73: 'tunc demum ad majora, quae supra commemoravimus, doctrinae virtutumque culmina Deo protegentes pervenies.'

76 Arno Schilson, 'Liturgy as the Presence of the Mysteries of the Life of Jesus according to Odo Casel,' *Communio* 29 (Spring 2002) p. 39.

reality of resurrection. Ontologically, this cultic juncture means 'being in Christ,' grafting ourselves into His humanity so that we can pass with Him to life in the Trinity.

> In the cultic mystery, the mystery of Christ becomes visible and effective; it is thus a prolongation and further unfolding of the *oikonomia* [salvation history or, better, the acts of salvation] of Christ, which, without the cultic mystery, could not transmit itself to all the generations of the community of the faithful spread throughout space and time.[77]

Casel develops the idea of the basic form of the liturgy as holy drama, a dramatic performance in which every participant is an actor, 'co-acting' with God.[78] Each one performs a grace-giving drama through which, by, with and through the Holy Spirit, each becomes "to a certain degree [Christ's] Person itself".[79] The question of how do we keep this possibility open at all times is answered by living liturgically which means embedding into the time/space structure of our lives an undergirding of song and praise which aerates the totality with a breath from elsewhere. This breath from elsewhere is the Holy Spirit. We gain access to this dimension by stretching the space-time warp of our lives across the framework of blessing, praise and thanksgiving, which is the daily schedule of the liturgy of the hours.

This I call keeping open the 'theandric' possibility inaugurated by Christ the Godman and maintained by Him, through the Holy Spirit. In Christ's resurrected state at the right hand of the Father, eternity and infinity can infiltrate our world. "Today if you should hear this voice,

---

77 Odo Casel, 'Glaube, Gnosis, und Mysterium,' *Jahrbuch für Liturgiewissenschaft* 15 (1941, pp. 115-305.

78 Odo Casel, 'Die Messe als heilige Mysterienhandlung,' in *Mysterium, Gesammelte Arbeiten Laacher Monche* (Muenster, 1926) pp. 29-52.

79 Odo Casel, *Die Liturgie als Mysterienfeier* (Freiburg, 1922) pp. 65 & 67.

harden not your hearts." Our freedom remains intact. The way we open this space is by opening our hearts and allowing them to become ventilators penetrating or seeping into the ground of time and space. Our time/space dimension is a second by second unfolding of chronology, so that the stance we take in the liturgy is up against the cliffside of infinity and eternity, which thereby can infiltrate and influence the inexorable droplets of history. Our job as monks is to hold open this ventilating system which allows a draught from 'the open' to invade our land. Doxology is the existential posture which allows the breath of the Spirit to transfigure the whole world. It also invites every element of creation to become the body and blood of Christ. Incarnation is not complete until that ultimate transformation takes place.

> At last they killed you and broke you in pieces while
> your sound kept lingering on in lions and boulders,
> in trees and in birds. There you are singing still.
>
> Oh you lost god! You inexhaustible trace!
> Only because you were torn and scattered through Nature
> have *we* become hearers now and a rescuing voice.[80]

Our *Opus Dei*, our liturgical schedule is the ritual sanctification of the hours of each day which eventually reach to the ends of the Earth.

As an anonymous community who gather in the church four times a day, we are thinning the air of pure human purpose so that the will of God, and thereby 'the kingdom of God,' can enter in. "O gates, lift high your heads, grow higher ancient doors, let him enter the King of Glory!"

To achieve this purpose we have to empty our hearts and lay them out like petals on a rose which "sleeps under manifold lids". We have

---

80   Rainer Maria Rilke, The Sonnets to Orpheus, Translated by Stephen Mitchell, Touchstone Books, Simon & Schuster, New York, 1986, p. 69.

to evacuate our egos and turn them into segments of a larger reality. This dethronement of the ego and abdication of our sovereign wills in favour of the container we create by such self-emptying is the way in which the incarnation of God can be continued and extended into the contemporary world, so that we too become the body of Christ. Our community is Rosicrucian Doxology – praise – thanksgiving – as a way of being – a stance – a posture – which uses the liturgy as a trellis or as a brace, a support system, to maintain this attitude.

'Jubilation' comes from the Latin for 'a wild shout': a cry that takes up the whole person into an explosion of breath. In the liturgy as we sing and recite the psalms, we breathe a column of air out in front of us, shaped by our bodies and our mouths as we form a choir. The song gives shape and colour to the pillar of sound as it moves between us and upwards. It gathers from each of us more than our intelligence or our ideas. It collects itself from the pit of the stomach and from a deeper, more comprehensive depth in ourselves. These depths are the feminine, creative, life-giving areas of ourselves.[81]

Another person living at the same time as Odo Casel who understood these realities and experienced this alternative dimension was the Austro-Hungarian writer, Rainer Maria Rilke. Widely recognised as one of the greatest German-language poets, his beautifully wrought and haunting images provide a much more attractive verbalisation of what it might mean to establish communion with God in an age of disbelief, solitude and anxiety.

....

81 Rainer Maria Rilke, Letter to a young woman, November 20th 1904: 'the deepest experience of the creative artist is feminine, for it is an experience of conceiving and giving birth . . . every poet has had that experience in beginning to speak.'

BEES OF THE INVISIBLE

René Karl Wilhelm Johann Josef Maria Rilke (December 4th, 1875 - December 29th, 1926), better known as Rainer Maria Rilke, travelled extensively throughout Europe (Russia, Spain, Germany, France and Italy), and in his later years settled in Switzerland. His writings include one novel, several collections of poetry and several volumes of correspondence. He lived in the same world around the same time as Odo Casel but his was a very different environment.

Rilke published the three complete cycles of poems that constitute *The Book of Hours* (*Das Stunden-Buch*) in April 1905, which explore the Christian search for God and the nature of Prayer, using symbolism from Saint Francis and his observation of Orthodox Christianity during his travels in Russia in the early years of the 20th Century.

Probably his most important works are the intensely mystical *Duino Elegies* which he began writing as a guest of Princess Marie von Thurn und Taxis at her castle in 1912. Aside from brief episodes of writing in 1913 and 1915, he did not return to this work until a few years after the war ended. He completed the collection in February 1922 while staying at the Chateau de Muzot in Switzerland's Rhone Valley. It was the news of the death of his daughter's friend, Wera Knoop (1900–1919), that inspired Rilke to create the *Sonnets to Orpheus* within a few days, between February 2nd and 5th, 1922. He later completed the following section of 29 sonnets in less than two weeks. These are the works which I hope will help me to articulate the thrust of this book.

"The driving force behind the cyclic composition of the *Sonnets to Orpheus* is to be seen in the ambition to create a whole system of meaning... as a result they not only refer to ancient mythology, but they also seek to take on the function once fulfilled by mythology."[82]

Rilke, as a poet, recognises that he can rescue objects from time by transforming them within, and expressing them in song. He discovers, through his poetic art, the ability to transform consciousness *and* world by having them interact in the poetic image.[83] In other words, his task is also a liturgical consecration. His poetry becomes a work of praise and transformation. In the *Sonnets to Orpheus*, Rilke takes Orpheus as the archetype of the inspired singer and the founder of all mystery religions, the first to reveal to us the meaning of initiation rites. Living like Orpheus or living the *Orphikos bios* (the Orphic way of life) means living the liturgical life of the greatest musician and poet of Greek myth. "Ultimately there is only one poet, that infinite one who makes himself felt, here and there through the ages, in a mind that can surrender to him."[84] When we reach the depth of singing we are no longer ourselves we become Orpheus, the one and only singer. "By the end of the book," Stephen Mitchell tells us in his introduction to the sonnets, "Rilke is no longer addressing Orpheus. He has become Orpheus, and can speak to his personal self from the centre of the universe. The cycle is completed. Life resolves in a single breath, and the tree of song that sprang up in the first line of the first sonnet is transformed into the serene, rooted 'I am' that is the Sonnets' last word, the word uttered at every moment by each particular form, and also the name of God."[85]

....

82 *The Cambridge Companion to Rilke*, Edited by Karen Leeder and Robert Vilain, Cambridge University Press, 2010, pp. 108-9.

83 Ibid. pp. 89-90.

84 Letter to Narmy Wunderly from Volkart, July, 29th 1920, quoted by Stephen Mitchell, op.cit. p. 164.

85 Rainer Maria Rilke, *The Sonnets to Orpheus*, translated by Stephen Mitchell, Touchstone, Simon & Schuster, New York, 1986, p. 10.

And where there had been
At most a makeshift hut to receive the music,

a shelter nailed up out of their darkest longing
with an entryway that shuddered in the wind –
you built a temple deep inside their hearing. [I,1]

This temple built inside our hearing is the liturgy of the hours. And Orpheus is both Christ and the Holy Spirit, the song of the interior fountain that wells up in our hearts.

And it was almost a girl and came to be
out of this single joy of song and lyre...
and made herself a bed inside my ear. [I,2]

A god can do it. But will you tell me how
a man can enter through the lyre's strings?
Our mind is split.

Simple, for a God.
But when can *we* be real?
Young man,
forget your own passionate loving and music . . .
True singing is a different breath, about
nothing. A gust inside the god. A wind. [I,3]

When Eurydice, the wife of Orpheus, died from a serpent's bite, he went down into the underworld to bring her back. His songs were so beautiful that Hades agreed to let her go back to Earth. The music of Orpheus could tame wild beasts and make rocks and trees move to his rhythm. Whenever we reach a certain depth with music that carries our praise and thanksgiving to ultimate depths, then it is always Orpheus who sings: "It is Orpheus once for all wherever there is song." Sonnet 7, Part One, is the most precise and vivid description of liturgical praise:

> Praising is what matters! He was summoned for that,
> and came to us like the ore from a stone's
> silence. His mortal heart presses out
> a deathless, inexhaustible wine.
>
> Whenever he feels the god's paradigm grip
> his throat, the voice does not die in his mouth.
> All becomes vineyard, all becomes grape,
> ripened on the hills of his sensuous south.
>
> Neither decay in the sepulchre of kings
> nor any shadow fallen from the gods
> can ever detract from his glorious praising.
>
> For he is a herald who is with us always,
> holding far into the doors of the dead
> a bowl with ripe fruit worthy of praise [I, 7].

In the *Sonnets to Orpheus* the second part of the cycle opens with the line "Breath, you unseeable poem", and in the subsequent lines the act of breathing is presented as an act of metamorphosis: absorbing the world (breathing in) and returning one's inner life (breathing out) represent an intimate exchange between the subject and the world: "ceaselessly, freely exchanging/ a measure of World for our being!/ Counterpoint, of whose rhythm I *am*." [II,1]. We can read the poem as 'visualised breathing', thus identifying the poetic text as the place of this intimate exchange between subject and world. This is the core of Rilke's Orphic concept: it is poetry that accomplishes metamorphosis, thus promoting human existence to a higher sphere: "true singing/ is whispering; a breath within the God; a wind" [I,3].

Breathing: you invisible poem! Complete
interchange of our own
essence with world-space. You counterweight
in which I rhythmically happen [II, 1]

We gain access to this dimension by stretching the space-time warp
of our lives across the framework of blessing, praise and thanksgiving,
which is the daily schedule of the liturgy of the hours. Living this dual
reality which Rilke calls "the whole", we are not meant to live up to a
timeless being, like God, or an eternal reality, like Heaven, or the promises
of any ideology, but rather we are to bear the timeless dimension of life
in mind while celebrating the moment. Our task is the metamorphosis
of the visible world with all its constraints into the realm of the invisible
as the key response.

'Tell the rushing waters: I abide.' [II, 29]
Inside the Double World
all voices become
eternally mild [I, 9]

Hail to the god who joins us;
for through him
arise the symbols where we truly live.
And, with tiny footsteps, the clocks move
separately from our authentic time.

This is our way of continuing the work of incarnation, the word being
made flesh, by becoming filters for the whole of creation until everything
is imbued with the breath of the Spirit. When we start the day liturgically
with an invitatory psalm: "Cry out with joy to God all the earth," we do
this on Earth's behalf. Praise is about inner marriage and outer marriage
in which we are the personal liaison. Inner marriage between us and God;

outer marriage between us and the world. Through this interconnection the Earth becomes consecrated.

All religion is made up either of symbols or activities mediated by symbols. Although many question the validity of abstracting some kind of general definition of religion from comparative study of those we encounter in every culture, it is surely possible to describe a phenomenon that is proportionately similar wherever we find it. It cannot be reduced to sociology or psychology although it has repercussions in both these spheres, it must be approached and studied as an autonomous instinct of humanity deserving of respectful examination in its own terms and right. "Religion might perhaps be defined, very generally, as belief in a fourth dimension – a dimension which takes us out of material space, where everything changes, disorder reigns, and we are lonely and unhappy, to attain *something which is*, a Being who exists absolutely, in all perfection and splendour. To feel that we are bound to that Being, that we are dependent on Him, to aspire to find Him, to hunger and thirst after Him: that is the religious sense."[86]

Even if adherence to religious institutions is in decline, our essential religious attitude has been maintained. 20th Century philosophers such as Jacques Derrida, who seem at the outset to be irreligious, are attempting to retrieve religion from 'the religions'.[87] The important thing is to salvage experience of the sacred from discredited institutions supposedly 'religious'. Religion, in the true sense, cannot be discarded "since it is part of the human experience and is something that is thrust upon us rather than something we choose for ourselves".[88] The Yellow-Eyed Hawk has urged us to put away all received beliefs and inherited suppositions and base all our knowledge on what is empirically verifiable; we have been

86 André-Jean Festugière, O.P. 'Personal Religion among the Greeks', University of California Press, Berkeley, 1954, Sather Classical Lectures, Volume 26, p. 1.

87 Jacques Derrida, 'Faith and Knowledge: The Two Sources of "Religion" at the Limits of Reason Alone,' in *Religion*, Jacques Derrida and Gianni Vattimo (eds), Stanford University Press, 1998.

88 David Tacey, *The Darkening Spirit*, Routledge, London, 2013, p. 28.

irretrievably shunted 'beyond belief' and there is no going back there in spite of the vociferous efforts of hardliners and fundamentalists; it is now necessary to base religious sensibility on an inherent mysticism which resides in each one of us and give birth to a new religious consciousness.

> Silent friend of many distances, feel
> how your breath enlarges all of space.
> Let your presence ring out like a bell
> into the night. What feeds upon your face
>
> grows mighty from the nourishment thus offered.
> Move through transformation, out and in.
> What is the deepest loss that you have suffered?
> If drinking is bitter, change yourself to wine.
>
> In this immeasurable darkness, be the power
> that rounds your senses in their magic ring,
> the sense of their mysterious encounter.
>
> And if the earthly no longer knows your name,
> whisper to the silent earth: I'm flowing.
> To the flashing water say: I am [II, 29].

Anthropologists and sociologists almost universally recognise the intimate relationship between religion and symbols. Clifford Geertz regards religion as part of a more universal cultural system. As cultural beings, we are symbolising creatures. He defines 'culture' as "historically transmitted patterns of meanings embodied in symbols — a system of inherited conceptions expressed in symbolic forms".[89] Religions

---

89 Clifford Geertz, 'Religion as a Cultural System,' in *Anthropological Approaches to the Study of Religion*, ed. M. Banton, Tavistock, London, 1966, p. 6.

constitute the institutionalisation of the general process by which a 'symbolic universe' is socially constructed and related to everyday social life. "Sacred symbols relate an ontology and a cosmology to an aesthetics and a morality."[90] This means that as human beings we are, more or less, programmed by our nature to devise for ourselves a satisfying explanation of the universe we were thrown into without our permission.

As monks, for instance, we cope with this existential reality by weaving with ourselves and for ourselves a magic carpet on which we can stand with security. This carpet is the liturgy, which forms a space/time machine on which we can negotiate the "slings and arrows of outrageous fortune". No one can understand this life unless they recognise that the primary work, the work of God, is a holding open four times a day, every day of the year, a space where God can be present in our world. By this work is created an alternative world. Liturgy enacts such a world where the hinted possibilities whispered by the Spirit can be given consideration. It sings the song of a world that is open to such possibility. Liturgy is cooperative world-construction. And it has to be done as a community. No one can perform a liturgy on their own. It is not the work of an individual. Each one of us has to give ourselves to the work as a silken thread that believes in the beauty of the carpet.

> Avoid the illusion that there can be any lack
> for someone who wishes, then fully decides: to be!
> Silken thread, you were woven into the fabric.

> Whatever the design with which you are inwardly joined
> (even for only one moment amid years of grief),
> feel that the whole, the marvellous carpet is meant [II, 21].

....
90 Clifford Geertz 'Ethos, world view, and the analysis of sacred symbols,' in *The Interpretation of Symbols*, Basic Books, New York, 1973, p. 127.

Those who celebrate the liturgy as the warp and woof of their existence can be compared to fire ants, a species called *Solenopsis invicta* which originated in the rainforests of Brazil. These ants, finding themselves thrown into a particularly rain drenched area, adapt to the region's frequent flooding by building rafts — made up of themselves. The fire ants connect by gripping each others' mandibles (appendages near the insect's mouth to grasp, crush, or cut the insect's food, or to defend against predators or rivals) and claws as we might lock shoulders together, which is similar to weaving a waterproof fabric. Half the ants get stuck underneath in a single layer — while the others form a chain mail covering on the top. The resulting two-layer raft is cohesive, buoyant and water-repellent. The ants down below can survive, thanks to tiny hairs on their bodies that trap a thin layer of air. These small pockets of trapped air prevent them from drowning. Roboticists interested in building self-assembling flotation devices are carefully studying their formation and techniques. Similarly, we overcome our propensity to drown in the chaotic world we find ourselves thrown into, by forming a choir and providing a landing-strip for the Holy Spirit. As the Prophet Zephaniah (3:9) says: "invoke the name of the Lord and serve him shoulder to shoulder". Our choir, our chorus (the Greek word 'Chora' defines the alternative space which we allow to happen in our liturgy, a space between and including this world and the next) which provides an opening through which the Holy Spirit can breathe into the world. We are guardians of this source of oxygen for the world. And we are not doing this for God, we are doing it for ourselves. "The Lord is my strength; the Lord is my song," we sing the Canticle of Moses. Without this strength we cannot survive; without this song we cease to exist. We are a singing people defined by our song. Song is our existence. Our liturgy together is the life-support machine we have established for ourselves as a body, according to our own rhythm of life, to enable us to maintain continual breathing contact with God. We need these prayer-stops to maintain equilibrium, especially in the morning. "In the morning let me know your love, for I put my trust in you. Make me know the way I should walk." (Psalm 142:8)

We alone of all the inhabitants of the Earth are capable of praise. Our task as human beings is to achieve the balance between the gravity of the Earth and the openness to the Spirit: the space between the within and the without. To live the 'outside,' to allow its breath to seep up through us so that we become its sound-box – this is what the Earth is asking of us.

> Yes the springtime did need you.
> Many stars demanded
> that you sense them. A wave
> long since gone by lifted itself toward you,
> or when you passed a window that was open, a violin
> gave itself up. All this was charge.
> But did you complete it?
>
> Earth, is it not this that you want: invisibly
> to arise in us? Is it not your dream
> to become one day invisible? – Earth! Invisible!
> What do you charge us with if not transformation?
>
> Earth, my love, I will. Oh believe me,
> Further springtimes are
> not required to win me-
> On my word, a single one, a single May
> is too much for my blood.
> I have been your
> tongue-tied subject
> for far too many years.

Rainer Maria Rilke, First Duino Elegy

Liturgy allows us to open ourselves to the 'presence' and to filter this through our bodies into the world; to allow this 'breath' to spread through us like a song. In this way liturgy produces honey from the rocks, from the secret places of the Earth. We can be compared to bees of the invisible when, through our liturgy, we make visible and palpable the reality, the presence of the other world, which secretes itself through our ritual into a luminosity or phosphorescence.

Walter Bruegemann has identified and nominated the particular stance, the precise posture, which marks liturgical co-creation. He calls it 'doxology,' the 'right way' to give praise to God. Doxology, or the liturgy of 'praise,' is not a response to a world already fixed and settled, it is participation in a world in the process of being decreed through this liturgical act. Wallace Stevens says: "It is certain that the experience of the poet is of no less a degree than the experience of the mystic and we may be certain that in the case of the poets, the peers of the saints, these experiences are of no less a degree than the experiences of the saints themselves."[91] This is why Rainer Maria Rilke's poetry is important as an expression of religious practice. Here is a quotation from a letter of Rilke himself:

> It can hardly be said to what degree a human being can carry himself over into an artistic concentration as dense as that of the Elegies and certain sonnets; often it is uncanny for the person who brought them forth to feel beside him, on the thinner days of life (the many!), such an essence of his own being, in its indescribable, ultimate weight. The presence of a poem like this stands out, in the strangest way, above the flatness and insignificance of daily life, and yet precisely out of that daily life was this greater, more valid existence wrested and achieved (how, the achiever himself hardly knows); for hardly has it been done before one again belongs in the general, blinder fate, among those who forget, or know as if they

---

91 Stephen Mitchell gives this quotation in his notes to the sonnets on page 158. It is taken from Wallace Stevens, *The Necessary Angel*, Knopf, New York, 1951, pp. 60, 50f.

didn't know, and who through an easy vagueness or inexactness help increase the sum of life's mistakes. In this way, every great artistic achievement, even to its furthest possible success, is both a distinction and a humiliation for the one was capable of it.[92]

92   Mitchell's translation pp.161-2 from a letter to Countess Mirbach, August 9th, 1924.

THE EUCHARIST FOR INSTANCE

What happens on the altar when we celebrate the Eucharist is a mystery. There have been many attempts to 'explain' what happens. Some make it sound like magic others try to make it pass for science. Both approaches are understandable and natural. However, the burden of my argument in this book is that we have to take the third way of truth, the Gospel truth, if you like, which is the only way to arrive at a satisfactory presentation of one of the greatest events in human history.

The Gospel words are startlingly simple: Unless you eat my flesh and drink my blood you shall not have life in you. And the night before He died Christ took bread, blessed it, broke it and gave it to his disciples saying: This is my body. And taking the wine He said: This is my blood. Do this in memory of me. Many then left Him because this was too hard a saying. When the disciples questioned Him and said do you mean this literally or can we interpret what you have just said symbolically, He more or less said take it or leave it – will you leave also?

How we explain this reality is a choice of language, of images, of metaphors. In both the Scriptures and the early Christian attempts to explain what happened, the way in which God set out to give us his life, the mystery of our salvation accomplished by, with and through Jesus Christ, myriad images are used: pastoral imagery, Christ as the Good Shepherd; military imagery, Christ as conqueror; medical imagery, Christ as healer; sacerdotal imagery, Christ as high priest; sacrificial imagery, Christ as lamb of sacrifice; and legal or juridical imagery, Christ as redeemer (coming from the word as used today for buying back what we have mortgaged). All of these are attempts to explain a mystery; none of them have either a monopoly or even pride of place.

So, we have the original event and now we have the present circumstances. A ritual in which these words are repeated over wine and a rather unrecognisable substitute for bread, and then where the least likely of these is distributed to the congregation and not the other, needs some vindication as replication either of what happened or as what was intended.

When you approach the altar and receive Holy Communion, as we say, you are not eating bread or drinking wine. There is more to it than that. However, neither are you eating flesh and drinking blood as such. To tell people, as I was told in my preparation for the sacrament, that you must not chew the host lest your teeth should stray and crush one of the toes of your saviour, is equally wide of the mark. Somewhere in between is the 'reality' involved in this mystery. And it is this in-between truth that is the subject of these pages.

The Middle Ages made a brave attempt both to understand and to explain the mystery. They called it transubstantiation. This was the very brilliant and subtle attempt of Thomas Aquinas, among others, to translate the mystery into the most appropriate formulae of his time. Eventually the Roman Catholic Church, even though hesitant and hostile at first, was so relieved and so impressed by the virtuosity and ingenuity of this succinct explanation that it declared it to have been divinely inspired and from that time forward anyone who did not believe in transubstantiation was a heretic.

I am not saying that the explanation wasn't brilliant for its time; nor am I saying that it is an unworthy or inadequate vessel for transmitting the burden of the mystery. What I am saying is that no formula can capture the mystery and that this particular formula, although it may have been useful as a convenient holdall at a time, has outlived its usefulness and has become doubly unhelpful in the 21st Century. I say doubly because on the one hand it is betraying the whole notion of mystery which is much more important to inculcate into the contemporary religious sensibility; and on the other because the whole philosophical framework within which it was originally enunciated has become obsolete. Scientific theory about matter over the last 300 years is incapable of taking seriously an explanation of anything in terms of accidents and substantial forms. So, in order to sell the total package today one has to first of all give the faithful a crash course in one of the most sophisticated and complicated metaphysical systems ever enunciated, and then get them to apply this to the 'concrete' situation of the Eucharist.

Aristotle saw the things of this world as composite. They were made up of matter and form, which, crudely speaking, was explained to people as the way a sculptor takes a piece of rock or wood (raw matter) and puts a form on it, although in the full treatment of Aristotle it was more subtle and complicated than this. Apart from this distinction, another which defined everything in the world that is, was the more difficult one of substance and accidents. Everything that is has a substance which could be described as 'an ultimate lump of stuff' that is the structure of its being, what underpins or undergirds (sub-stare = to stand underneath) it. Accidents are the other part of its composition and these are what we are able to apprehend with our senses. The volume, the shape, the size, the colour, the taste, the texture of anything is an accident. This is an unfortunate word because it means in philosophy something entirely different to what we normally think of when we hear the word. The car crash, the broken limb, the smashed teacup, the fall on ice: these are accidents in our vocabulary. For the inventors of the transubstantiation formula, accidents were all those things which accrued to a substance and which our senses were able to detect. What we could see, hear, touch, taste, smell of anything at all had to be an 'accident'. So, it was almost as if everything had two layers one substantial and the other accidental.

So, the first thing one had to do when explaining the 'mystery' of the Eucharist to anyone who wanted to be a Catholic was to give them the rules of the game they had to play. You explained to them about substance and accidents. You told them that everything they could see or touch or taste was an accident but that underneath these sensory data there was another reality which we call the substance. Then it was an easy move to explain what happened when we were celebrating the Eucharist. After the words of consecration when the priest (and it had to be an ordained priest, because anyone else would not have the power) had elevated the 'elements' of bread and wine, these particles of the created world were changed into the body and blood of Our Lord Jesus Christ. This happened, not at the level of accidents, which we could see or verify, it happened at the deeper level of substance to which no one had access. But if you were a Catholic you could 'see' with the eyes of faith that what was now on the altar was no longer bread and wine but the body and the blood of Jesus Christ.

Contemporary physics has replaced the whole theory of substances with the more dynamic notion of atoms, molecules, neutrons, electrons etc. which is just as mysterious to most people. It is now suggested to us that the 'substantial' world we imagined was around us and which, indeed, we kept painfully bumping into, was in fact a deceptive bundle of ever-shifting particles which danced before our eyes like hordes of mosquitoes, masquerading as solid tables, chairs and other apparently substantial props within our domestic horizons. So, again for most of us, the second equally unconvincing 'explanation' at least had the effect of questioning the other's infallibility.

There is also no doubt that Aquinas had a different understanding from Aristotle of the substance/accident amalgam, infused as this was by his understanding of creation and of God as creator. So few people in the world today are conversant with either Aristotelian or Thomistic philosophy, it seems somewhat far-fetched to propose either of these great thinkers as appropriate tutors to 21st Century believers. Catherine Pickstock, professor in the faculty of divinity at the University of Cambridge, is one of those who does know what she is talking about in this sphere. She gives a contemporary account of this understanding in her book *After Writing* which has the very apposite subtitle from the point of view of my argument: *On the Liturgical Consummation of Philosophy*. She understands Aquinas as saying that every particle of creation is, in fact, transubstantiated and that what happens in the Eucharist is only an extreme case of what happens all the time in terms of our existence here on Earth.[93]

Just as the redness of a button on my coat can be 'substantial' in terms of the button, but 'accidental' in terms of the coat, so all creatures participate 'accidentally' in Being when placed in the context of God's creation although they may appear to be 'substantial' in themselves.

All bread is essentially 'accidental' in the sense that it derives its 'substance' from its being assimilated into bodies of one kind or another, it has no substantial reality in and for itself. As transubstantiated 'free-floating accidents' bread and wine can become "directly sustained by their participation as particular contingent created things in the *esse* of the divinely transfigured human body to which they are conjoined".[94] But in this they are simply repeating what has already happened from the beginning of time to every particle of creation through Christ, the word, "the lamb who has been slain since the beginning of the world" (Rev 13:8).

The Eucharist also is Christ as He is and as He always has been from the beginning: as the fullness of everything and the only and inexhaustible source of life. In other words Christ has always been and always is nothing less and nothing other than the gift of the Eucharist, and the whole world

---

93 'Hence every creature is "pulled" by its participation in *esse* beyond its own peculiar essence – it exceeds itself by receiving existence – and no created "substance" is truly substantial, truly self-sufficient, absolutely stable or self-sustaining. It follows that the violation of the substance/accident contrast and the gap between *esse* and essence in the case of transubstantiation is only an extreme case of what, for Aquinas, always applies. All substances are "accidents" in contrast to divinity, and become signs which, in their essence, realise a repetition and revelation of the divine "substance" (although Aquinas finds even the category of "substance" to be inadequate for God). Catherine Pickstock, *After Writing: On the Liturgical Consummation of Philosophy*, Blackwell Publishers, Oxford, 1998, pp. 260-261.

94 Ibid. p. 260.

in every possible particle of it is always potentially a eucharistic element.[95]

All of this suggests that the word 'transubstantiation', understood within the context of a metaphysics that is intellectually viable, can be used as a valid way of 'explaining' the mystery. However it should not be imposed as an acceptable, still less as a prescribed, way of explaining the mystery which takes place in the Eucharist for people who have no initiation into the rarefied thought-forms which undergird its coherence. Such a metaphysical framework is really of little interest to people living in the 21st Century and who hunger for the reality which the Eucharist has to offer. The 21st Century must find its own way both of describing what is happening and of encouraging people to take part. No explanation is sufficient, no formula can capture the mystery, but the notion that we should cease from exploration and rely simply on an attempt made in the 14th Century is both cowardly and suicidal. Cowardly because it shirks from the responsibility to promote; suicidal because such reliance on an obsolete explanation could ensure the demise of Eucharistic practice altogether.

In 1972 a rugby team was flying over the Andes mountains when their plane crashed. Those who survived were stranded without food or shelter on a snow-capped peak. Two of their teammates died in the crash. They had no means of communicating with the outside world and had no hope of being rescued. No one knew of their whereabouts or realised that their plane had gone down. Eventually they were forced to cut up and eat the bodies of their dead friends. They described the horror and the difficulty which this decision caused and yet how they were

---

95 "If the Eucharist repeats what was in the first place a repetition, then it repeats Christ as Himself always nothing other than the gift of the Eucharist. This Christology is most fully expressed in St John's Gospel, whose prologue was often recited at the Last Gospel, by the Priest and Ministers during their recession or unvesting at the end of the Mass in the medieval Roman liturgy. In this Gospel, the Logos is described as *pleroma* – that is, as fullness, an inexhaustible source of life. He is at once everything and more than everything, and yet, in the Johannine story, he is present through testimony and supplementation. Paradoxically, Jesus is the fulfillment of all signs, and yet is only revealed through a series of signs.' Ibid. pp. 264-265.

driven to it by starvation and determination to survive. When eventually they were rescued and their story began to leak to the press, the whole world was appalled by this display of what they called cannibalism. The survivors were vilified as monsters and vampires. However, when these young and very ordinary people eventually appeared on television screens and told their story and when they said that this experience made them really understand what was meant by the words 'this is my body' which they had heard all their lives in terms of the Eucharist, then public perception was altered.

When you think of it, they must have meant exactly what some people believe when they are taking the Eucharist. A convert friend of mine says he became a Catholic because he saw actual blood in the chalice in a Catholic Church. Such a literal translation has been condemned by the Church and those who gave grisly descriptions of how they were chewing muscle and sinew were declared to be heretics or insane. So, let's face it – we are not saying that.

On the other hand, we are not saying that the bread and the wine are simply replacing the body and blood either as symbols (transsignification) or as capsules (consubstantiation) we are insisting that in between these two possibilities: eating flesh as a cannibal eats flesh and eating bread as a meat substitute which can also act as a reminder of what someone wonderful did for us, there is a third kind of truth and this is what we call the 'sacramental' reality, reminding ourselves that 'sacrament' is the Latin translation for 'mystery'.

There is a quantum leap in the poetry of Gerard Manley Hopkins between what he wrote before 1875 and what he wrote after that year, which critics have explained variously from excoriated sensuousness to manic depression of a cyclothymic kind.[96] My view is that Hopkins might have been a somewhat second-rate Victorian poet in the manner of Swinbourne or Rossetti if he had not undergone the acid bath of Roman

....

96 Norman White quotes this view from a letter he received from William Sargant, an eminent psychiatrist, in his book *Gerard Manley Hopkins in Wales*, London, 1998, p. 150.

Catholicism and Jesuit discipline. And I say more, if Hopkins was saved from an inferior, predictable, romantic poetry by the Roman Catholic Church, in a further and more crucial step, he was saved by poetry and language itself from a maudlin triumphalist Roman Catholicism which is everywhere irritatingly present in his prose and more self-conscious poetry.

It was in 1872 that he received the 'revelation' through his reading of the theology of Duns Scotus, which was the realisation that the beauty of God and the beauty of the world are not contrary opposites but rather participations in one another. The notion that Hopkins later called 'inscape' was essentially a mystical insight that all ontology is essentially inherent Christology, if one has the eye for the essential.

One of the theological dogmas that caused Hopkins to leave his own denomination and become a Roman Catholic was the real presence of Christ in the Eucharist, technically referred to as transubstantiation, whereby the bread and wine on the altar become the body and blood of Christ. Duns Scotus allowed him to extend this intuition to the whole of creation. Every fragment of creation is potentially a Eucharistic element and Hopkins now saw his vocation as a priest/poet to make such sacraments available to God's people. This revelation was 'a mercy from God' who, through it, had now given Hopkins 'His leave' to both examine the beauty of the world around him and to express it. The journal entry for August 1872 that records this new discovery conveys something of his excitement and relief: "Flush with a new stroke of enthusiasm. It may come to nothing or it may be a mercy from God. But just then when I took in any inscape of the sky or sea I thought of Scotus."[97]

Hopkins was studying theology from 1874 to 1877, the year of his ordination to the priesthood, and during this comparatively happy time at St Beuno's in Wales, he developed this 'merciful intuition' into a highly refined understanding of the mystery of God's real presence in

---

97 *The Journals and Papers of Gerard Manley Hopkins*, ed. Humphrey House and Graham Storey, London, 1959, p. 221.

this world. The poem which is most successful as an incarnation of the 'lovescape' he apprehended in the world is 'The Windhover'. Here he achieves his version of transubstantiation through word and rhythm in a liturgy "to Christ our Lord". The Windhover is a poetic deed, a Eucharistic sacrament, which Hopkins told Bridges was one of the best things he had ever written. This, in sonnet form, is Hopkins' theological vision, the mystery of the Trinity, and his most perfect expression of that for which he forsook everything in his life, the Real Presence of God in our world. In a letter to Bridges he says that "It is the true mystery, the incomprehensible one" which we cannot explain "by grammar or by tropes" but which, for convinced Catholics, "leaves their minds swinging; poised, but on the quiver".[98] In this poem Hopkins discharges his mission. His sonnet is not 'about' the Windhover, it is the Windhover. At no moment does he interject his homiletic tendency or pedagogy. His heart remains in hiding. He elaborates "a great system and machinery" to "catch" the bird and transubstantiate it into the real presence of the one to whom the poem is dedicated. Hopkins knew that A.D. had rendered metaphor anachronistic. The word must be made flesh. The word must be and not be about. This poem also achieves seamless unity between poet, language and thing. The poet is incarnate in the poem, not aloof, explaining or preaching. Everything in him and the inscape of the bird "flush and fuse the language":[99]

> God's utterance of himself in himself is God the Word, outside himself is this world. This world then is word, expression, news of God. Therefore its end, its purpose, its purport, its meaning, is God and its life or work to name and praise him.[100]

....

98 Letters to Bridges. *The Journals and Papers of Gerard Manley Hopkins*, op. cit. pp. 186-188, letter of October 24, 1883.

99 *The Sermons and Devotional Writings of Gerard Manley Hopkins*, edited by Christopher Devlin S.J. London OUP, 1959, p. 129.

100 Ibid. p. 129

Hopkins' language is strange and his poetry is difficult because it is theological vision put into words. He knew that this was what his vocation was and what his language was for. He wrote, almost obstinately to Bridges (April 1st, 1885) "If you do not like it [my music] it is because there is something you have not seen and I see. That at least is my mind, and if the whole world agreed to condemn it or see nothing in it I should only tell them to take a generation and come to me again."

It is a mystical vision which becomes available to the reader through the techniques of the poetry and the contemplative capacity of the beholder. "My heart in hiding/ Stirred for a bird, - the achieve of, the mastery of the thing!" The poem is the ingenius mediator between the inscape of the 'thing' and 'instress' in the reader. The '*haeceitas*' of the particular falcon is revealed in all its glory by the achievement of the poem. 'A bird' is X-rayed through to its sacramental propensity to represent the real presence of the Trinity:[101]

> Suppose God showed us in a vision the whole world enclosed first in a drop of water, allowing everything to be seen in its native colours; then the same in a drop of Christ's blood, by which everything whatever was turned scarlet, keeping nevertheless mounted in the scarlet its own colour too.[102]

'The Windhover' articulates such a vision except that "here" the whole world is enclosed in the windhover itself, as a particular bird, "seen in all its native colours". Then "the same" is seen in "a drop of Christ's blood", as "gold-vermilion". The work of the Holy Spirit is to achieve the conjunction, the hypenation of what I am and what Christ is, without

101 Ibid. p. 194.
102 Ibid. p. 194

spilling a drop of the native colour of either.[103]

....
103 I have given a more extensive account of the poetry of Hopkins in my book *Anchoring the Altar*, Veritas, Dublin, 2002, pp. 112-146.

PART V

INVOKING IRELAND

I take the title[104] of this chapter from John Moriarty [1938-2007] who gave his life and his work to salvaging the mythological dimension. The year before he died, he was planning to set up a 'hedge school'[105] where people would be introduced to this liturgical way of knowing and alternative road towards truth. "What we have in mind" the optimistic brochure outlined, "is a Christian monastic hedge school for adults that will be called Slí na Fírinne." This will start us on "an adventure, great and dangerous, in Christian living". "This isn't flight" he assures us, "it is serious engagement otherwise and elsewhere."

Bob Geldof in TV programmes called *A Fanatic Heart* to mark the centenary of the Irish uprising in1916 made a provocative statement:

> One hundred years ago, a handful of Irishmen and women rose up against the British Empire. A six-day rebellion ended in their execution and elevation to near-sainthood. But are they Ireland's greatest heroes? Is the GPO Ireland's most sacred place? To me, it represents the birth of a pious, bitter and narrow-minded version of Ireland I couldn't wait to escape. But there was another version of Ireland, dreamt up by a poet… His vision was mythical, romantic, truly heroic and beautiful. That was the Ireland I could never leave

....

104 John Moriarty, *Invoking Ireland*, Dublin: Lilliput Press, 2005.

105 "Formerly in Ireland, in the absence of state education for their children, people would come together and build a school. Typically, it would be a mud hut completed in a day and it was here that someone having himself some attainment in education, would set up as a teacher, charging his pupils a penny a day when and if they could afford it." John Moriarty, *News* from Slí na Fírinne, Autumn, 2005.

behind. As Gogarty said, 'there is no Free State without Yeats'. By which he meant that Ireland doesn't exist without the poet.

Both Denis Donoghue and Morton Irving Seiden[106] suggest that W.B. Yeats' poems were seen by him as a kind of liturgy.

> The basic assumption is that souls do not die and therefore may be evoked. Correspondingly, the *anima mundi* is not merely a store of images and symbols, it is what a race dreams and remembers. The great soul may be evoked by symbols, but spirits are not mere functions of ourselves, they have their own native personalities. So the best reading of the *anima mundi* is that it is the subjective correlative of history, a nation's life in symbols; it is not our invention, but may respond to our call, if like the mage we speak the right words. He must go on perfecting earthly power and perception until they are so subtilised that divine power and divine perception descend to meet them, and the song of earth and the song of heaven mingle together.[107]

Yeats saw great art in general, and his own poems in particular, as embodiments of the supernatural. His symbols have theurgical power; his poems and plays are sacred rites. "In a number of his essays, but notably in 'Speaking to the Psaltery', first published in 1902, he urges that his poems be chanted or intonated as though they were (it seems) Orphic prayers." By means of these supernatural poems "he tried to recreate in the modern world the mythologies of ancient India, Eleusian Greece, and pre-Christian Ireland".

In 1977 Richard Kearney and I founded a journal called *The Crane*

....

106 Morton Irving Seiden, *The Poet as a Mythmaker 1865-1939*, Michigan State University Press, 1962, pp. 286-7.

107 Denis Donoghue, *We Irish, Essays on Irish Literature and Society*, University of California Press, 1986, pp. 35 –51.

Bag partly with the intention of promoting such mythic intelligence in Ireland. We explained this intention in the first editorial:[108]

> The Crane Bag is really a place. It is a place where even the most ordinary things can be seen in a peculiar light, which shows them up for what they really are. There must be a no-man's land, a neutral ground where things can detach themselves from all partisan and prejudiced connection and display themselves as they are in themselves. Does such a place exist? Can such a place exist?

We went on to elaborate: Modern Ireland is made up of four provinces, whose origin lies beyond the beginnings of recorded history. And yet, the Irish word for a province is cóiced, which means a 'fifth'. This five-fold division is as old as Ireland itself, yet there is disagreement about the identity of the fifth fifth. There are two traditions. The first that all five provinces met at the Stone of Divisions on the Hill of Uisneach, which was the mid-point of Ireland. The second that the fifth province was Meath (Mide), the 'middle'. Neither tradition can claim to be conclusive. What is interesting is that both divide Ireland into four quarters and a 'middle', even though they disagree about the location of the middle or 'fifth' province. This province, this place, this centre, is not a political position. In fact, if it is a position at all, it would be marked by the absence of any particular political and geographical delineation, something more like a dis-position. What kind of place could this be?

In Ireland one may still be confronted with the riddle: 'Where is the middle of the world?' The correct answer to the riddle is 'Here' or 'Where you are standing'. Another version of the same idea is the division: North, South, East, West, and Here. "The figure five is the four of the cross-roads plus the swinging of the door which is the point itself of crossing, the moment of arrival and departure."

....
108 *The Crane Bag*, Vol 1, no 1, Spring 1977, p. 3-5.

Uisnech, or the secret centre, was the place where all oppositions were resolved, the primeval unity. The discovery of points where unrelated things coincide was always one of the great arts of seers, poets and magicians. Thus, the constitution of such a place would mean that each person must discover it for themselves within themselves. Each person would have to become a seer, a poet, an artist. The purpose of *The Crane Bag* is to promote the excavation of unactualised spaces within the reader, which is the work of constituting the fifth province. From such a place a new understanding and unity might emerge.

In Volume II, 1978, devoted entirely to 'Mythology,' we asked the question: "Is there an alternative way in which Irish people can develop and cultivate a sense of identity?" We were trying to introduce a specific understanding of mythology.[109] It was an ineffectual attempt to introduce people to an alternative language, a middle voice, somewhere between scientific and historical fact and unbelievable fantasy. An interview with Paul Ricoeur conducted by Richard Kearney in Paris that same year, 1978, and included in *The Crane Bag*, suggested the following:

> Scientific language has no real function of communication or interpersonal dialogue. It is important therefore that we preserve the rights of ordinary language where the communication of experience is of primary significance. But my critique of ordinary language philosophy is that it does not take into account the fact that language itself is a place of prejudice and bias. Therefore, we need a third dimension of language which is directed neither towards scientific verification nor ordinary communication but the disclosure of possible worlds. This third dimension of language

109 *The Crane Bag Book of Irish Studies (1977-1981)*, Dublin, Blackwater Press, 1982, p. 155.

I call the mytho-poetic. The adequate self-understanding of [hu]
man[kind] is dependent on this third dimension of language as a
disclosure of possibility.[110]

Truth as a disclosure of possibility was our theme. The title of our journal
was borrowed from *The Crane Bag and other Essays* by Robert Graves. His
title essay is a review by himself of a book by Dr Anne Ross called *Pagan
Celtic Britain*. Hers was a book intended to explain to the general public
the meaning of its title. Graves believed that this highly qualified academic
Celtologist is barred from understanding the very material she is writing
about because of her university education and scientific mentality. "As a girl
of seventeen Dr Ross had done what anthropologists call 'field-work' by
learning Gaelic for six months in a West Highland peasant's hut. Then after
graduating at Edinburgh, she took an educational job in the same Goidelic
region, but later returned to Edinburgh for a degree in Celtic studies and a
Ph.D. in Celtic archaeology." Thus, according to Graves "she forgot . . . how
to think in Gaelic Crofter style, which means poetically".

He makes his point by quoting her treatment of an important Celtic
Myth about 'The Crane Bag' of the sea-god Manannán Mac Lir. This
bag had been made from the skin of a woman magically transformed
into a crane. "This crane-bag held every precious thing that Manannán
possessed. The shirt of Manannán himself and his knife, and the shoulder-
strap of Goibne, the fierce smith, together with his smith's hook; also the
king of Scotland's shears; the King of Lochlainn's helmet; and the bones
of Asil's swine. A strip of the great whale's back was also in that shapely
crane-bag. When the sea was full, all the treasures were visible in it; when
the fierce sea ebbed, the crane-bag was empty."

Graves maintains that Dr Ross, like the rest of us, has been trained out
of poetic sensibility. She has lost the art of reading the signs of the times.
She "can make nothing of such fairy-tale material". He has to interpret

110 *The Crane Bag Book of Irish Studies (1977-1981)*, Dublin, Blackwater Press, 1982, p. 266.

for her: "What the fabulous Crane Bag contained was alphabetical secrets known only to oracular priests and poets. The inspiration came, it is said, from observing a flock of cranes, 'which make letters as they fly'. The letters are formed against the sky by the wings, legs, beaks and heads of these shapely birds. Hermes, messenger to the Gods, afterwards reduced these shapes to written characters. Cranes were in fact totem birds of the poetically educated priests... That the Crane Bag filled when the sea was in flood, but emptied when it ebbed, means that these Ogham signs made complete sense for the poetic sons of Manannán, but none to uninitiated outsiders. The Crane Bag was not, in fact, a tangible object, but existed only as a metaphor." Dr Ross, as an academic archaeologist, has the job of digging up 'things' from the past, dating and comparing these. But as a trained scientist "she can accept no poetic or religious magic". Anything that falls outside the scope of her "academic conditioning" is "branded as mythical – mythical being, like Pagan, a word that denies truth to any ancient non-Christian emblem, metaphor or poetic anecdote". Such is the point of view of the mythologist.

This analysis was attacked by Alan Tucker in *The New York Review of Books* of October 1967. He accuses Graves of being antiquarian, prejudiced and ignorant: "Perhaps the most distressing thing about Graves' article is his clear anti-academic, anti-intellectual bias. There is no reason at all for his condescending treatment of Professor Ross's field work (sneer), education and research (chortle), except as an attempt to gull his readers into the outdated belief that myths and 'magical materials' require visceral, rather than cerebral, understanding." He continues in the same vein elaborating an alternative approach to mythological thinking:

Unfortunately there are still those who feel they can apprehend the meaning of ancient myths through some sort of spiritual communion with long-dead ancestors; I have seen the same done in archaeology. And all too often these people have a fixation to which all myths must eventually revert: Graves' bag is not the Crane, it is Greece. But despite his contempt for academic mythologists, and especially archaeologists, it is these professional students who for years have laid the foundations upon which hacks can build their castles in the air.

Note the reference to "academic mythologists" as opposed to those "building castles in the air". There is only one idiom available to scientists, archaeologists and mythologists alike; there can be no specific idiom for the truth of myths as a discipline in itself. To which Graves replied in the same edition:

My piece about the Irish God Manannán's Crane Bag [*NYR*, June 29] annoyed scientific archaeologists because I suggested that their task was to dig, photograph, preserve, and date new finds rather than to pronounce on their religious character: a special field reserved for those few anthropologists who happen to be poets as well... The same piece encouraged a leading Jungian to sermonise in rotund eighteenth-century style on the esoteric, as opposed to the exoteric, meaning of the Sea-God Manannán's Crane Bag. Dr Jung, however, was neither a trained anthropologist nor a poet, but a psychologist. What he called the unconscious - a term first coined by my German great-grandfather, the "Natur-philosoph" Gotthilf von Schubert - is what poets regard as the true conscious: a composite of those deeper levels of consciousness upon which they draw while in their active, waking, creative trance.

Graves continues to applaud himself for his interpretation of the Crane Bag myth: "An immediate, if modest, instance of deep-level consciousness was my casually reading the Crane Bag passage quoted in Dr Anne Ross' *Pagan Celtic Britain* and finding an immediate poetic answer to its complex system of kennings which nobody, so far as I know, had been able to decipher since medieval days."

And so an aggressive confrontation between two different idioms continues without hope of reconciliation. Mythos "...tells us of events that are real not in the sense of having happened just like that, but in the sense of being the kind of thing that is always happening. Real as history is, it is finally less true than myth. Myth is always and forever true; actual history is never more than an approximation of the truth of life."[111] Myths are cryptographs of the great design and pattern of human history. The Odyssey, the Exodus, were two kinds of journey which every human being makes, one where you go out and come back, the other where you go out and keep going. Each one is etched into the contours of our being human. Mythology is not a series of random stories but the very fabric of the soul.[112] This 'poetic' form of consciousness, this kind of knowledge, which we are calling 'mytho-poetic', has every right to exist, to be cultivated, promoted, and valorised, as much as the mathematical and geometrical way of thinking. It is not a question of denying the value of mathematical and scientific knowledge. It is rather a question of reinstating another kind of knowledge which is equally important and *sui generis*.

The 'Mytho-Poetic' could be specifically and connaturally a Celtic way of being in the world. Our island is small and self-contained enough to provide an object lesson and a case history of mythological landscape. Every acre of each province is a geography of lived folklore. Holy mountains, sacred hills, fairy forts, ancient trees, healing wells, are to be found in settings second to none in terms of natural beauty. From the islands of the Skelligs to the Giants Causeway and the cliffs of Moher, sea, sky and countryside combine to provide a living stage for mythological weavings that have continued and been recorded since humans first inhabited these shores. Artists of every kind have recognised and represented these dimensions in ways that provide an all-embracing psychic memory now embedded in the rocks. Their 'embroidered cloths'

....

111 David Tacey, *Religion as Metaphor, Beyond Literal Belief,* Transaction Publishers, New
    Brunswick, 2015, p. 29.

112 Ibid. p. 45.

are maps which show what no ordnance survey or satellite picture can convey. Every vista in every province is potentially an opening to such alternative worlds. Tell the stories which surround the places in which we live and the countryside comes alive.

Since the beginning of the 20th Century [and the founding of our Free State] we swapped British Rule for three alternative colonisations: a particular brand of 'nationalism'; a homegrown blend of 'Catholicism'; and the prevailing Western culture of 'scientific realism'; and we set sail into the century at breakneck speed. One hundred years later, when all three 'isms' have worn thin, we might go back to the beginning and examine the footprints to review the alternative routes we mostly avoided at the time; and, above all, to gather the riches that, in our hurry, we may have left behind.

Imagination is always and already huge in children, you only have to release it, encourage it, guide and direct it. And not too prescriptively either. Just let the flowers blossom of their own accord. Imagination, to borrow a phrase from Alan McGlashan,[113] is "a golden key that is the careless plaything of all children, and the conscious instrument of a few geniuses". Imagination is what we should be cherishing, encouraging, cultivating, instead of which we are systematically deleting it from the desk-top of every child who wants to get enough points to enter our third level institutes of education. This country should be and could be an incubator of the imagination, a role model for others. And the truth is that, as teachers, we don't have to do anything. Creativity is already there – as Picasso says: "every child is born an artist".

113 Alan McGlashan, *Savage and Beautiful Country: The Secret Life of the Mind*, Hillstone, New York, 1966, p. 11.

CELTIC BRAINWAVES

As Celts, living on this island of Ireland we should revive those secret ways in which our ancestors aligned themselves with the natural cycles and eternal destinies which offer us at least some of our specific dignity as human beings. Medieval monks have left us an account of Irish history that allegedly extends back to nearly 3000 BCE. Before the 17th Century, when the Yellow-Eyed Hawk was introduced, this history might have been accepted as a generally accurate account of how things happened in the past. However, in the 21st Century everything in these accounts which date further back than the 5th Century is "dismissed as *fabula*, the product of a wild Irish imagination".[114]

> I have walked and prayed for this young child an hour,
> Imagining in excited reverie
> That the future years had come
> Dancing to a frenzied drum
> Out of the murderous innocence of the sea.
>
> Oh, may she live like some green laurel
> Rooted in one dear perpetual place
> How but in custom and in ceremony
> Are innocence and beauty born?
> Ceremony's a name for the rich horn,
> And custom for the spreading laurel tree.[115]

....

114 .P. Mallory, *In Search of the Irish Dreamtime, Archaeology & Early Irish Literature*, London, Thames & Hudson, 2016, p. 59.
115 William Butler Yeats, 'A Prayer for my Daughter'.

Ceremony, ritual and custom, these are aboriginal ways of inhabiting the earth. They help us to establish ourselves, inserting us personally into the maelstrom, at "the point of intersection between the inward adventure and the outward continuum that we live".[116] Connecting the inward adventure, the twenty, thirty, forty, fifty, sixty, seventy, eighty, ninety, even a hundred years which may be given to us to live out our lives here on earth, connecting that to the outward continuum, those millions of years during which the earth has been in motion, such is the target. We have cut away this indigenous part of ourselves in an attempt to become modern, up-to-date, economically competitive. We should go back to living our dreamtime if we wish to re-inhabit an essential part of ourselves, rediscovering the meanings which lakes, mountains, hills, and streams, for instance, might offer to our dreams. Where do such meanings come from? From the dreamer's personal experience of life, certainly. But, also from the meanings attributed to such things by the culture in which we grew up. Lakes, mountains, hills, and streams, "carry implicit meanings for all members of our species, codified in our brains and psyches as a consequence of having evolved in the environmental circumstances typical of this planet".[117]

Children of the 21st Century were forced to put away these ambitions and these dreams, for one reason or another, and simply required to grow into ordinary men and women. How did this happen? We have been subjected to a debilitating and diminishing educational system. Schumacher in his book *Small is Beautiful* suggests that "if Western civilisation is in a state of permanent crisis, it is not far-fetched to suggest that there may be something wrong with its education".[118]

Jill Bolte Taylor, an American neuroanatomist, began to study severe mental illnesses because she wanted to understand what makes the brain

116 Eavan Boland, *Object Lessons, The Life of the Woman and the Poet in Our Time*, New York, Norton, 1995.

117 Anthony Stevens, *Ariadne's Clue, A Guide to the Symbols of Humankind*, 1998.

118 E.F. Schumacher, *Small is Beautiful*, London, Abacus edition, Sphere Books, 1974, pp. 64-66.

function the way it does. Her brother was schizophrenic and she wanted to know how and why her dreams were such an important and inspiring part of her reality, whereas her brother could not connect his dreams to reality, without making them delusional. She began working in a lab in Boston where they were mapping out the brain to try to understand which cells communicate with which. On December 10, 1996, she herself had a stroke. A blood vessel erupted on the left side of her brain, causing a major cerebral haemorrhage in that left hemisphere. She was able to witness her own brain being shut down. Within a span of four hours, she could not speak, read, walk, write or remember anything from her life. She compares her stroke to being like an infant again.

Her personal experience of this massive stroke, in 1996 when she was 37 years of age, and her subsequent eight-year recovery period, are the subject of her book *My Stroke of Insight, A Brain Scientist's Personal Journey*, published in 2006. "Although we experience ourselves as a single person with a single consciousness," she has personal and scientific knowledge and experience of "the two very distinct characters cohabiting my cranium... the two halves of my brain [which] don't just perceive and think in different ways at a neurological level, but they demonstrate very different values based upon the types of information they perceive, and thus exhibit very different personalities". Many of us speak about how our head [left hemisphere] is telling us to do one thing while our heart [right hemisphere] is telling us to do the exact opposite... Jill Bolte Taylor came to the understanding that: "at the core of my right hemisphere consciousness is a character that is directly connected to my feeling of deep inner peace. It is completely committed to the expression of peace, love, joy, and compassion in the world."[119]

In a book called *The Broken Harp, Identity and Language in Modern Ireland*, biologist and author Tomás Mac Síomóin suggests that the Irish people have had a similar experience to Jill Bolte Taylor at a cultural level.

....
119 Jill Bolte Taylor, *My Stroke of Insight*, London, Hodder & Stoughton, 2008, pp. 132-3; 146.

He presents the decline of the Irish language as one of the most insidious outcomes of the multi-faceted colonisation of the Irish people from the 16th Century to the present day. He sees Irish history as a closing down of the Irish mind in a process initiated by the Tudors, perpetuated by the Irish Catholic Church who, moving to occupy a power vacuum created by the end of the Irish War of Independence, served to consolidate the English-imposed status quo.

The particular psychological profile of the Irish as a people who, for generations, had suffered genocide, famine, and sexual crime, as consequences of these first two waves of colonisation, engendered in us, according to this author, a catastrophic vulnerability to the third and present wave of colonisation, which is Anglocentric neo-liberal globalisation.

The only way to recover from these three 'strokes' and retrieve our natural and accustomed way of thinking and being, according to Tomás Mac Síomóin, is for all of us to make the effort to return to speaking Irish, which would readjust our brains and help us to regain our identity.

This is possibly a plausible hypothesis, but I for one don't see it happening. We are essentially a pragmatic people and what's happened has happened and I do not see us, as a people, making the huge effort required to reinstate Irish as our mother tongue. As Bill Bryson remarks: "All the evidence suggests that minority languages shrink or thrive at their own ineluctable rate. It seems not to matter greatly whether governments suppress them brutally or support them lavishly. Despite all the encouragement and subsidisation given to Gaelic in Ireland, it is spoken by twice as many people in Scotland, where there has been negligible government assistance." This view is confirmed in the recent Cambridge History of Ireland which states: "Notwithstanding many inducements, financial resources and patriotic exhortations, the decline of Irish has continued."[120]

---

120 Thomas Bartlett, *The Cambridge History of Ireland, Volume IV, 1880 to the Present*, Cambridge University Press, 2018, p. xxxiii.

Although some may see it as a tragedy, I, for one, am grateful to have English as my mother tongue. The language of Shakespeare and Joyce allows me to express myself accurately and adequately, and to communicate with huge numbers of people throughout the world. That this happened through colonial oppression in the past doesn't make it any less advantageous to the present. To quote Bill Bryson again, as an objective outsider:

> We naturally lament the decline of these languages, but it is not an altogether undiluted tragedy. Consider the loss to English literature if Joyce, Shaw, Swift, Yeats, Wilde, Synge... and Ireland's other literary geniuses had written in what is inescapably a fringe language... No country has given the world more incomparable literature per head of population than Ireland, and for that reason alone we might be excused a small, selfish celebration that English was the language of her greatest writers.[121]

I don't believe it is practical or even desirable to reinstate Irish as our first language, although it certainly is a route to first-hand acquaintance with the roots of our identity. There is an umbilical connection between the ancient language of Ireland and the very geography of the island. The Irish language is one of our most precious treasures, more so than all that is contained in the National Museum, or all the museums of the world; let us guard it scrupulously, use it generously, and make of it a source of local pride and global enrichment; but let us not use it to make any one feel alienated, belittled or ashamed. Language should be a major storehouse for culture. But, it is no longer our 'first' language, and it has ceased to be our vernacular language. We should neither pretend that it is, nor try to impose it as such; it is our umbilical language, our

121 Bill Bryson, *Mother Tongue: The Story of the English Language*, Penguin Books, London, 1991, pp. 36-37.

secret connection with the body of the land. Those privileged few who inhabit it as their native tongue are our interpreters, our oracles in times of decision, our sources of connection with the ground of our being. But they are not everything and neither are we. We both need each other to make our way forward in an ever expanding universe where the legacy of the local must feed the galaxy of the global.

And we have in fact made English our own, sometimes with a rage and ferocity that has mangled it out of recognition. We have gnashed our teeth so persistently and effectively in English that we have at times reduced it to its bleeding gums. German experts suggest that it is because of the various strokes we suffered culturally, our being cut off from our mother tongue and forced to adopt an alien one, that we seek to emphasise our speech by using the epithet 'fuck' as one might sprinkle chilli powder on baked beans. These German experts see us as the worst offenders in this regard in the whole of Europe. It has got to the point now where young Irish people are not just saying fuck before and after every word, but they are cutting the words in two and saying 'abso-fucking-lutely'.

On television and radio programmes, however, we still follow BBC protocol, introducing a beeper whenever the word is used on air. This is, perhaps, feasible in the less extravagant or flamboyant landscape of Great Britain but in the present incarnation of English in the Republic of Ireland it becomes 'beebeepulous'. In a documentary programme on leadership qualities, for instance, the late great Paídi Ó Sé was followed into the changing room to discover how he was able to galvanise the Kerry football team into such insuperable action before every all-Ireland final. The beeper goes epileptic. 'Put the ***ing ball, *** it, in the ***ing net.' Etc.

The Abbey Theatre, founded in 1903 by WB Yeats and Lady Gregory, sees its mission as "creating world-class theatre that actively engages with and reflects Irish society". For most of its Irish repertoire you can put away your beeper and fasten your safety belt. Irish plays in the English language rarely bypass a fuck on whatever road they are travelling.

The theatre of Tom Murphy has been spoken of as "a holy theatre, a search for soul in a soulless world, a theatre of the possible, a theatre of the spirit". His language is a search for images, symbols and myths that will, once again, enable us to tell the story of who we are. I quote from himself, offstage:

> I've been told my characters tend to be harsh but if that's so, the harshness is only there because they feel they have been betrayed somehow or that they have betrayed something in themselves.

> *Whistle in the Dark* I wrote on Friday and Saturday nights with my feet up in the kitchen - I used to notice that my jaw was frequently clenched - there was some sort of rage within me, and I had found a form of therapy to deal with it, which was trying to write a play.[122]

What J.D. Salinger was to the 1950s Roddy Doyle is to the 1990s and beyond. *The Commitments* or *The Snapper*, without exaggeration, have the word fuck in some shape or form on every page. In his 1993 novel *Paddy Clarke Ha Ha Ha*, Roddy Doyle climbs into the mind of a 10-year-old boy from Dublin in 1968. This boy would be about 50 years old today. He is full of admiration for an older boy who plays soccer and is his hero.

> I wanted to be like Charles Leavy. I wanted to be hard. I wanted to wear plastic sandals, smack them off the ground and dare anyone to look at me. Charles Leavy didn't dare anyone; he'd gone further than that: he didn't know they were there. I wanted to get that far. I wanted to look at my ma and da and not feel anything. I wanted to be ready...

....
122 *Bomb* 120, Summer, 2012, Tom Murphy interviewed by Colm Tóibín.

He said Fuck like - I wanted to say it exactly like him. It had to sound like no other word sounded, quick and sharp and fearless... His head shot forward like it was going to keep going into your face. The word hit you after his head went back. The Off was like a jet going overhead; it lasted forever. The Fuck was the punch; the Off was you gasping.

Fuck awffffff.

With Joyce we have a descent into the boiler room of language that goes beneath any of our particular dialects. This is the uncovering of language as that gesture of being which establishes a new dimension of humanity. *Finnegans Wake* is an attempt to articulate a language adequate to our situation, by digging up the letters from the dump-heap of the world: the mystery of the 'root language' that holds 'the keys of me heart'.[123] European civilisation, represented by the mythic figure of Finn, is restored to life (again) but this time a(wake): so you have *Finnegans Wake*: Finn again awake - the rebirth of our ancient mythology in a language deeper than either English or Irish. It is an attempt to recover the 'mytho-poetic' dimension. "Yet is no body present here which was not before. Only is order othered. Nought is nulled. Fuitfiat!"[124]

For what was the Western world except a projection of the human mind as both these realities were understood. Such understanding was short-sighted. It took our conscious minds as its vantage point and used language as a servant to this cause. Now language comes as a tidal wave from the unconscious, not something 'out there' and available for use, like an overcoat or a briefcase, but like an everflowing river that runs through us, and through all the ages of our history. The river will, if we

....

123 FW 626.
124 FW 613.

listen to it, whisper to us the secret of our origins, while at the same time it will wash away the architecture of a world built without adverting to it. The artist of language in this capacity is the guardian and shepherd of being as it expresses itself through the traces of all recorded human utterance, the anatomy of language:

> ...when the call comes, he shall produce nichthemerically from his unheavenly body a no uncertain quantity of obscene matter... with this double dye brought to blood heat, gallic acid on ore, through the bowels of his misery,... the first till last alshemist wrote over every square inch of the only foolscap available, his own body, till by its corrosive sublimation one continuous present tense integument slowly unfolded all marryvoising moodmoulded cyclewheeling history...[125]

The artist of such a language does not fly in a cerebral fashion over the forest of words, he situates himself in the thick of the jungle and hacks away at the roots of syllables until he reaches that 'root language' which holds "the keys of me heart".[126]

Language is the main character in *Finnegans Wake*. Starting with the very particular European city of Dublin and the particular life of an individual author, the generative power of language leads the artist into an underworld of the universal unconscious, much as the entry into any particular subway station will lead down to that network of underground correspondences which connect with every other one.

The Wake of this universal dimension requires the sleep of ordinary language and the daytime logic of the cerebrospinal cortex. The "stomach language" has to be "nuzzled over a full trillion times forever and a night... by that ideal reader suffering from an ideal insomnia"[127] who has to forget

---

125 FW 185-6.
126 FW 626.
127 FW 120.

the way he was taught to read, and allow language to become the "aural eyeness"[128] which will provide the "keys to dreamland".[129]

This new kind of poetry which is *Finnegans Wake* is a recreation of the myth of European humanity. It provides a restratification of the order of values as these had been developed at every level from philosophy to art. It shows a new way of communicating from the mytho-poetic which is between the conscious and the unconscious, an alternative way of knowledge between fantasy and fact, between proof and fiction, a 'middle voice', a 'third language.'

128 FW 623.
129 FW 615.

ONE WAY TRAFFIC ON *SLÍ NA FÍRINNE*

John Moriarty was born in North Kerry in 1938. He showed early promise at school in Listowel before going to University College, Dublin, where he gained a double-first in philosophy and English literature. He was widely regarded as having one of the finest minds of his generation. On page one of his book *Slí na Fírinne* published in 2006, the year before he died, John tells us: "Of someone who has died, we say in Irish, *tá sé, tá sí ímithe ar shlí na fírinne,* meaning that he, that she, has set out on the path or trail of truth".

After a couple of years, John went to the University of Manitoba, Canada, where he taught English literature for a further eight years.

When the first 700 pages of his autobiography appeared in the year 2000, Paul Durcan hailed it as "one of the most remarkable autobiographies I have ever read in my entire life... every household in Ireland should have a copy of this magical book". And Aidan Carl Mathews called it "the greatest book since *Ulysses*".

When Brendan Flynn introduced John's work to Anthony Farrell, and the Lilliput Press published his first book *Dreamtime* in 1994, Jeff O'Connell wrote in *The Galway Advertiser* on the 3rd November that year:

> Even dreams need some clarity... Here we have a style which is either bafflingly obscure, self-consciously riddling, or maddeningly repetitive, and sometimes all at the same time. His is an oracular style that seems to erect barriers behind which his meaning hides. There is no virtue in such wilful obfuscation, especially as the content of what he is trying to say is both timely, important and profound... Perhaps what I am trying to say is that it seems unfair to lob this book at someone without respecting and taking into

account the 'strangeness' anyone in our materialistic, scientifically mesmerised civilisation will have with it. Moriarty's essential project is seriously flawed... by this failure of style.

This is the enigma of John Moriarty. If I take one paragraph from *Nostos*, which, for me, summarises the philosophical intuition underlying Moriarty's thesis, and if I supply it with some footnotes which he was unprepared to submit, it may clarify somewhat the overall project.

A more enlightened Enlightenment will suggest that our *Discourse on Method*[130] is not a sufficient substitute for the *Mabinogion*,[131] nor is our *Principia Mathematica*[132] a sufficient substitute for a *Principia Mythica*.[133]

....

130 René Descartes autobiographical and philosophical treatise of 1637 which caused a revolution in epistemology. Its full name is *Discourse on the Method of Rightly Conducting One's Reason and of Seeking Truth in the Sciences* (French title: *Discours de la méthode pour bien conduire sa raison, et chercher la vérité dans les sciences*). The *Discourse on The Method* is best known as the source of the famous quotation: "Je pense donc je suis." ['Cogito ergo sum'. 'I think therefore I am']. One of the most influential works in the history of modern philosophy, and important to the development of natural sciences, Descartes started his line of reasoning by doubting everything, so as to assess the world from a fresh perspective, clear of any preconceived notions.

131 The earliest prose stories of the literature of Britain. The stories were compiled in Middle Welsh in the 12th–13th Centuries from earlier oral traditions. They offer drama, philosophy, romance, tragedy, fantasy and humour, and were created by various narrators over time. The title covers a collection of eleven prose stories of widely different types. The stories are so diverse that it has been argued that they are not even a true collection. The word *mabinogi* itself is something of a puzzle, although clearly derived from the Welsh *mab*, which means "son, boy, young person".

132 The landmark work in formal logic written by Alfred North Whitehead and Bertrand Russell published in three volumes in 1910, 1912 and 1913. Written as a defense of logicism (the thesis that mathematics is in some significant sense reducible to logic), the book was instrumental in developing and popularizing modern mathematical logic.

133 Such does not as yet exist, except as a title for John Moriarty's life and work: *The Return to Mythica*

A Principia Mythica we will continue to have only when someone is willing to live it, or be lived by it, myth after myth. In this regard Aeschylus[134] is exemplary, for he doesn't only retell the myths as he finds them. In retelling them he harrows them and he therefore also harrows the assumptions on which our culture is founded. Sometimes of course no amount of harrowing will suffice, for, faced with consequences, we come to see that what we need are new myths that imagine and validate new ways and these we either import or beachcomb the shores of unconsciousness for.[135]

Moriarty allowed himself to live mythologically and to be lived by it myth after myth. This is why the two enormous volumes of his autobiography contain more stories from the archives of various cultures

....

134 Greek playwright (525/524 – c. 456/455 BC) often described as the father of tragedy, only seven of his estimated seventy to ninety plays have survived. The roots of Greek drama are in religious festivals for the gods, chiefly Dionysus, the God of wine. The *Oresteia* trilogy concentrated on man's position in the cosmos in relation to the gods, divine law, and divine punishment. Michael Ewans argues in his *Wagner and Aeschylus: The Ring and the Oresteia* (London: Faber. 1982) that the influence was so great as to merit a direct character by character comparison between Wagner's *Ring* and Aeschylus's *Oresteia*.

135 John Moriarty, *Nostos, An Autobiography*, Dublin, The Lilliput Press, 2001, 2011, p. vi. *Nostos* is an ancient Greek word a theme used in Greek literature which includes an epic hero returning home by sea. It is a high level of heroism or greatness. This journey is usually very extensive and includes being shipwrecked in an unknown location and going through certain trials that test the hero. The return isn't just about returning home physically but also about retaining certain statuses and retaining your identity upon arrival. Homer's Odyssey is the paradigm. Nostos can be told by those who experienced it themselves. Achilles, who never experienced a Nostos could say: "my nostos has perished, but my kleos will be unwilting". In this instance, he has chosen the route of glory and says he will not now return home because it is destined that he will die in battle. Odysseus [Ulysses] was able to tell his own story of his nostos since he has survived. Nostos meant several different things in this epic, it meant escaping death, safe landings, returning home from war, and being back home. The word 'nostalgia' was first coined as a medical term in 1688 by Johannes Hofer (1669-1752), a Swiss medical student. It uses the word νόστος along with another Greek root, άλγος or algos, meaning pain, to describe the psychological condition of longing for the past.

than from his own personal experience. Every incident of his life leads into an experience already recorded in the annals of human existence in one culture or another. Instead of relying upon personal memory and the hunt for accuracy as in Proust's *Remembrance of Things Past*, Moriarty ransacks the wardrobe of universal mythology to clothe each memory of his own biography in the borrowed robes of previous experience. Always in the recorded dreamtime of some however unacknowledged cultural heritage there is a pattern or an adornment to suit the trembling experience that each of us imagines to be happening to us for the first time. When we see these experiences superimposed against the backdrop of universally recorded human experience in general, we begin to appreciate the depth of weave in what we are presently going through and we expand our own horizons accordingly. What was it that allowed John Moriarty so naturally to accede to this mytho-poetic dimension? There can be many explanations on offer.

Brian Lynch reviewed Nostos in *The Irish Times*, Saturday, 17th March, 2001. This review was so remarkable that I quote from it somewhat lengthily:

> There is a thread to the narrative... : sex. Or rather, Moriarty being perhaps the quintessential Irishman of the mid-20th Century, sex and the family... But where is the sex? Moriarty's answer, I imagine, is that it is everywhere in the book, including the places where it is not... all of which is a roundabout way of saying that Moriarty has, and knows that he has, a deep-seated fear of emasculation. I say he knows he has it – 'in a kind of Eucharistic despair we drink the blood of our own castration' – but how well he knows it is another question. He certainly refers to it often enough, linking it explicitly to a memory of his mother cutting the head off a cock (well, yes) and seeing the blood spurting between her thighs into a bowl. But, apart from being a deliberately chosen theme – old Father Jung looms large – does he know how profoundly this dread informs the rest of the history?

Sexual anxiety can be used to interpret Moriarty's inability to form lasting relationships, his hermeticism, his dualism (extraordinarily Eurocentric); it is also useful in making sense of his style, or rather tone of voice: babbling, baby-brilliant, obsessional, essentially nervous... Thus a poor little Kerry boy with a fear of losing his 'Titanic bollocks' grows into an almost androgynous god, a chattering Christ.

This is very brilliant and very perceptive, but as Mary McGillicuddy says in her introduction to the life and thought of Moriarty, it is "not the whole story".[136] To my mind, the key moment in John's life and the one during which he was forced to articulate the meaning of his work, was when he decided to give up his highly paid job in Canada. He was uncomfortable as an academic and decided to give up all the security and the benefits which such a life can ensure in order to return to Ireland where he was basically unemployed for the rest of his life. Why did he leave such a promising job within sight of being tenured? The following quotation brings us to the crux:

> 'Puberty has caught up with me,' I said. 'There is a sexual puberty and, however shyly or hesitantly at first, most of us learn to go with it. As well as this sexual puberty, however, but altogether more demanding than it, there is another kind of puberty – for the moment and with good reason I'm refusing to call it a spiritual puberty – but whatever it is, or will turn out to be, I am yielding to its claims, I am going with it... It is a question of recognising our deepest yearning – let us forget about our desires, our desires only serve to muffle and hide our deepest yearning from us – and, having recognised our deepest yearning, we then go on and so set ourselves up that we can live from it and with it... I sensed

---

136 Mary McGillicuddy, *John Moriarty: Not the Whole Story*, Dublin, Lilliput Press, 2018.

or something greater than me sensed that our deepest yearning doesn't have who we individually and empirically are in mind."

"Sounds selfish to me," he said.

"And possibly egotistical. I've acknowledged that. But then, was it either egotistical of us or selfish of us to have gone with our first puberty. Surely, for most of us at any rate, we had no choice?" [*Nostos* p. 397].

What was this Rubicon in John's life - John Moriarty's Passover to another world? He almost called it "spiritual puberty". Most tribes mark it with some rites of passage, because they understand it to be such a gigantic step that it needs a mythological backdrop to prepare us for the journey. The goal of the second half of life should be to realise [that is 'to make real'] your other half, your spiritual as well as your bodily personality. In terms of your sexuality, for instance, the purpose in the second half of life is not to propagate the species but to give birth to the soul, which for many of us is the most difficult birth of all. Crossing the divide between youth and age has become for our culture a journey of mythic proportion. We are facing as never before a spiritual crisis. This is what John Moriarty discovered and he made every effort possible to introduce us to this fact.

At spiritual puberty everything that we have, everything we do, everything we are, has to be transposed to another plane, and the language for this is mythological and the world we enter is symbolic.

'How can someone be born when they are old?' Nicodemus asked Jesus when he visited him by night, as recounted in the third Chapter of John's Gospel. 'Surely they cannot enter a second time into their mother's womb!'

Jesus replied, 'Very truly I tell you, no one can see the kingdom of God unless they are born again of water and the Spirit. Flesh gives birth to flesh, but the Spirit gives birth to spirit.'

'How can this be?' Nicodemus asked.

'You are Israel's teacher,' said Jesus, 'and do you not understand these things?' .

That was John Moriarty's question to the academics of this world? How can you not understand what is really the most important thing? Modern society is paying a high price for abandoning the symbolic life, whether this was encased in a religious or a spiritual framework. Without any such cultural or religious outlet, the psyche will resort to pathologies to express its interior life and impulse.

Mythic intelligence, which was John Moriarty's gift, weaves its way through symbols and has a very different perspective on the universe to that of the scientist.

The purpose of Moriarty's work is to introduce people to an ancient language, an alternative truth, somewhere between scientific fact and unbelievable fantasy. It could be described as a middle voice with some of the characteristics of the other two, but carrying in itself a distinct identity. Between fact and fiction there is a sliding door, a place of imbrication, which means an overlapping of edges allowing for spaces between. Mythic intelligence is not something childish to be discarded as we grow up; it is an essential part of human understanding. The language of myth is specific; it carries a particular truth of its own. This language has a different logic from the one we are used to in our everyday world. Poetry becomes the natural idiom of such truth. That is why poets have recognised so immediately the genius of John Moriarty.

Nostos is not just a return journey for him; it is a return journey for us. His work, *Invoking Ireland* was trying to bestir us into salvaging the mythological dimension.

Every culture has access to this underground transport system. The stories may be coloured with national costume and local dyes, but the shapes and structures are recognisably similar, the geometry of the story obeys planetary rules. We are in the territory of the universally human and our petty idiosyncrasies fade as we expand with the horizon. John Moriarty became fluent in such language and the range of his facility was breath-taking. He set out to uncover an alternative route towards truth. He regained for us a forgotten right-of-way almost defunct from lack of use. He tried to show us how to live symbolically and metaphorically.

SWEENEY ASTRAY

In 1996, Seamus Heaney was Emerson poet in Residence at Harvard. Emerson had spoken of America as "a poem in our eyes; its ample geography dazzles the imagination". He called on Americans to produce a poet to lend it "metres". Seamus Heaney saw Emerson's point. He used geography through poetry "to shape and give palpable linguistic form to two kinds of urgency - one symbolic, one explicit".[137] In one kind of survey all that is required of the map is topographical depiction: diagrammatic representation of an area of land or sea showing physical features. In the other someone's heart provides an extra compass. Heaney's poetry introduces us to such "double vision", which detects in the visible traces of the invisible. Especially in his 1991 volume, *Seeing Things* (Faber & Faber), Heaney shows us, on his "journey back/ into the heartland of the ordinary",[138] particular realities in our world which act as portals to the unknown, windows on the invisible, doorways into the dark, "a half-door/ opening directly into starlight".[139] Looking at water carved in stone on a cathedral façade, the poet sees a hidden world conjured by the sculptor's art. Stone provides durability; art invokes the subtlety.

> *Claritas.* The dry-eyed Latin word
> Is perfect for the carved stone of the water
>
> . . .
>
> On the facade of a cathedral. Lines
> Hard and thin and sinuous represent

137 *The Crane Bag Book of Irish Studies (1977-1981)*, Dublin, Blackwater Press, 1982, p. 155.
138 Seamus Heaney, *Seeing Things*, London, Faber, 1991, p. 7. This poem 'The Journey back' was not included in Seamus Heaney, *Opened Ground, Poems 1966-1996*, London, Faber, 1998.
139 Seamus Heaney, *Opened Ground, Poems 1966-1996*, London, Faber, 1998, p. 384.

The flowing river. Down between the lines
Little antic fish are all go. Nothing else.
And yet in that utter visibility
The stone's alive with what's invisible:

All afternoon, heat wavered on the steps
And the air we stood up to our eyes in wavered
Like the zig-zag hieroglyph for life itself.

Earth, fire, air and water, the elements of our world can become "zig-zag hieroglyphs for life itself". Heaney is high-priest of such mythopoetic utterance, developing a language, an alphabet and a vocabulary to allow us bestride both worlds:

'The English language/ belongs to us...
'... it's time to swim
out on your own and fill the element
with signatures on your own frequency,
echo-soundings, searches, probes, allurements,
elver-gleams in the dark of the whole sea.'[140]

The title of Heaney's Nobel Lecture in 1995 was "Crediting Poetry".[141] He would 'forge' a connection between the world we experience around us and another world which he had been brought up to call "supernatural". Heaney would reject the presentation of such a world which his religion outlined as a dogmatic belief structure, and he would meticulously explore and redefine in his own words the possibility of such connection. His religion of birth and his literary vocation were at odds in this domain,

---

140 Heaney, *Opened Ground*, p. 267-8.
141 The lecture is printed in *Opened Ground*, pp.. 447-467.

and one of his tasks was to come to terms with such antagonism.[142]

Heaney is pushed or guided towards an encounter which is not mediated through Irish Catholicism, but which happens without the need of any intermediary through direct mystical contact with the Divine, the possibility of achieving transcendence without having to employ any of the locally available transport systems. This is Heaney as "a latter-day and revised Stephen Daedalus forging a conscience of rural Catholic Ireland – even more, of rural Catholic Northern Ireland".[143] The metaphysics to which Heaney's poetry introduces us is not 'beyond' [as the word 'meta' means in Greek] the physical world in which we live; it is a dimension of that very world itself. Nor is it 'above' the natural world as words such as 'supernatural' might imply. It may not be readily visible to us who live so avidly and one-dimensionally in this world, but that does not mean that it is not situated squarely within. Access to it is achieved by learning its language, that middle voice of the mytho-poetic, "freshening your outlook/ beyond the range you thought you'd settled for,"[144] "where the extravagant / Passed once under full sail into the longed-for".[145]

This last line could be a description of mythological thinking.

142 "I was wanting to write about contemporary Ireland, the Republic of Ireland, as a country with a religious subconscious but a secular destiny - at the point of transition from the communality of religious devotion to the loneliness of modernity and subjectivity. The community in the poem has lost the sense of its own destiny and of any metaphysical call." Here Heaney is talking about his poem, 'The Mud Vision' from the collection The Haw Lantern [1987] [cf. Opened Ground, Poems 1966-1996, London, Faber, 1998, p. 321] in the 1997 interview, The Art of Poetry No 75, The Paris Review, No. 144, Fall 1997.

143 Ibid. pp. 168-9.

144 Ibid. p. 383.

145 Seamus Heaney, Opened Ground, Poems 1966-1996, London, Faber, 1998, p. 390.

CONCLUSION

The argument being put forward in this book is that there are two complementary but distinctive ways of 'reading' the world we live in. We need some middle term between myth [interpreted as fantasy] and history. My suggestion here, borrowed from Ricoeur and others, is that mytho-poetic intelligence, which is between the conscious and the unconscious in ourselves, could provide an alternative epistemology between fantasy and fact, a 'middle voice,' a 'third language.' It is a perfectly valid and very ancient way of thinking and being. It was the only and preferred way of most cultures of the past; it was the way of thinking of those authors who created our scriptures and these are not accessible unless we approach them in this way. It is not, as some have held, an outdated stage in the history of consciousness, but a vitally important exercise of consciousness which has an in-built niche in the very structure of consciousness. This is not to decry technological advance, nor is it to deny the perfectly logical and legitimate language of science. It is suggesting that certain countries of Europe [Greece, Norway, Ireland, for instance] are conservatories of mythology and could develop this way of thinking as a complementary parallel to the dominant culture of the West at this time.

Ireland, along with Greece and the Scandinavian countries [all with vast mythological archives] could provide a haven for this part of ourselves. Religion belongs to this dimension. We could provide for Europe, and for the world, an oasis in the desert of unilateral thinking. We can do this quite naturally. Just as Finland and Hungary have developed an educational system which valorises and promotes music wherever that muse inspires any of their students, so Ireland could focus specifically on imagination as one of its natural assets. Such cultivation of the right half of the brain, linking the heart and the head in a full-blooded epistemology could co-exist with first-class emphasis on neo-cortical achievement and all the subjects which work best from that area of the brain. Ireland could become a mythological sanctuary which would provide a natural landscape for those wishing to taste and see and hear this alternative reality, not just for antiquarian or tourist delectation, but as essential 'dreamtime' for anyone hoping to live a fully integrated and comprehensive human life.

More books from the Author

The Opal and the Pearl

(COLUMBA BOOKS, HARDBACK, €19.99) ISBN: 9781782183068

With seven billion human beings on one planet we need a new ethics guiding us in our way of relating to one another sexually. Author Mark Patrick Hederman critiques Catholic teaching on sex, and stresses the need for an ethics of sexual behavior outside the very specific and particular demands of heterosexual marriage. The message of artists has been consistent: 'we cannot be reduced to any formula. We have to accept the blood-and-guts reality of what we are. We need to be human, fully human and any ethics must provide for us as such.'

Five Years to Save the Irish Church

(COLUMBA BOOKS, PAPERBACK, €9.99) ISBN: 9781782183518

Many believe the death knell of the Catholic Church in Ireland has been sounded. This is the time for radical change. Including speeches from a national conference hosted by Columba Books in May 2018, *Five Years to Save the Irish Church* is a clarion call from some of the most respected and challenging religious commentators of our time. Using their extensive experience in working for a better Church and society, the authors of this book offer a game plan to revive the Irish Church and help it transition into a more honest and open Church.

All books are available to order directly from www.columbabooks.com

More books from the Author

Underground Cathedrals

(COLUMBA BOOKS, PAPERBACK, €14.99) ISBN: 9781856076951

'My proposal is that, at this time, the Holy Spirit is un-earthing an underground cathedral in Ireland which could help to replace the pretentious, over-elaborate Irish Catholic architecture of the twentieth century.'
Coupled with very incisive and honest comments on the current state of the church, and with a reflective medita-tion on the Murphy Report on the Dublin Archdiocese, Abbot Hederman offers a visionary and very stimulating image of how things might be if only we all listen to the voices of artists in our midst.

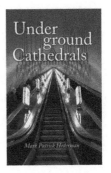

Dancing with Dinosaurs

(COLUMBA BOOKS, PAPERBACK, €9.99) ISBN: 9781856077354

Dinosaurs have been described as the most successful ani-mals that ever inhabited this planet. We had to learn how to live with them, and survive in spite of them. Today we have invented our own dinosaurs. Churches, banks and multinationals are some of the modern breed of dinosaur. Small may be beautiful, but in the world in which we live it is not very durable. Unless any organisation becomes a dinosaur it will not survive the vicissitudes of history.

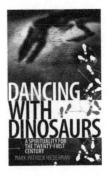

All books are available to order directly from www.columbabooks.com